Phoenix in Perspective

Reflections on Developing the Desert

Phoenix in Perspective

Reflections on Developing the Desert

Grady
Gammage Jr.

The Herberger Center for Design Excellence
College of Architecture and Environmental Design
Arizona State University

The Herberger Center for Design Excellence
College of Architecture and Environmental Design
Arizona State University, Tempe, AZ 85287-1905

Mary R. Kihl, Ph.D., AICP
Director/Associate Dean for Research

Audrey Brichetto Morris, Editor

Book design by Brenton Elmore

Book layout by Kingston Communication Art

Cover photos: aerial courtesy Todd Photographic Services
                 ranch house by Matthew Gammage

Photographs by the author unless otherwise noted.

The Herberger Center's publishing activities are made possible by
an endowment from the Herberger family to the Arizona State
University Foundation.

Printed by G&G Printers. Printed on 80# Accent Opaque smooth.

Contents

Foreword

The perspective of Phoenix offered in this book is the view of an insider. Grady Gammage Jr. was born here, has spent most of his working life as a lawyer here, and has been a heavily engaged community leader. This book is the second in a series published by the Herberger Center for Design Excellence of the College of Architecture and Environmental Design at Arizona State University. We call the series Phoenix Dialogues. The first was written by an eminent local architect, Vern Swaback, who gave his book the title *Designing the Future*. He also is an insider, having spent most of his career based in Scottsdale and at Taliesin. Our goal has been to support the efforts of leading members of this community to share their experienced and considered views about this extraordinary place we call the Valley of the Sun, and in particular to share their opinions about a constructive and creative future for this rapidly expanding Sonoran Desert city.

A couple of years ago Grady came to me with an idea that I found to be both hugely gratifying and quite surprising. He was thinking about taking a six-month sabbatical from the day-to-day demands of his busy and successful law practice, and he suggested that our College might provide the haven within which he could sit back and think hard about the issues confronting his community and his role in it. We already knew Grady well, indeed he has taught in our School of Planning and Landscape Architecture and has been a good friend, both personally and of this College. I don't know whether it was his idea or mine, but the decision to record those reflective thoughts in a book that we might publish clinched the deal for me. And now I have had the pleasure of reading it.

The publication date of these writings could hardly be more timely. Over the last few years greater Phoenix has been experiencing an explosive growth, the like of which it had not known for over 20 years. The impact of this growth has alarmed the community as it sees its valued desert lands disappearing under the blades of the bulldozers and replaced by a sea of red tile roofs atop the stucco walls of houses in ever-larger sizes on ever-smaller plots, each lot surrounded by a six-foot high concrete block wall to protect the swimming pool. Desert landscaping is modestly reintroduced, but rarely in a scale and quantity that will support the idea of living at one with the desert.

Sprawl is the word that is attached to this phenomenon, and it includes the innumerable retail centers at arterial crossroads, where cars stack up as they produce the brown cloud that, on a winter's day, conceals the mountains that form the Valley of the Sun.

"Smart Growth" is the call from Governor Hull and the legislature as they attempt to identify a direction for the future that will reconcile the forces of economic growth and development with the pressure from the citizenry not to destroy the assets of desert landscapes, brilliant light, views to the mountains, and the unique sense of place and lifestyle that have brought so many here.

As an insider, Grady Gammage Jr. is not persuaded by the simplistic remedies he hears offered. Draconian growth limits, high residential densities, severe financial penalties on new development, and vast mass transit schemes are not for him. He knows too well how deep the roots are of the existing patterns of growth to be persuaded that such radical changes of direction are either appropriate or reasonable.

A significant part of this book is an account of how the metropolis assumed its current form and pattern. Water and the car are primary shapers. And it is those issues to which Grady returns. For him, water, not land, is the resource that defines this place, and it is our decisions about water usage that will shape our plans for the future. Automobiles, for him, will remain the primary mode of transportation, but they need to be augmented by appropriate mass transit where it makes sense, and adapted to the new technology of electric vehicles for shorter, repetitive trips.

A big question remains, which is, "What will be the ultimate impact of asynchronous electronic communication?" Telecommuting and changes in commuting patterns hold out opportunities and expectations as radical in their own way as the impact of the car on trolleys and trains in the 1940s.

Grady Gammage Jr. has accepted the challenge to be constructive, and so toward the end of this remarkable book there are a series of carefully considered, but ambitious, recommendations. It is not my task here to preempt his arguments, or spill the beans on his punch lines, so I will instead urge the reader to follow the arguments of this skilled writer as he reaches conclusions and recommendations based on a lifetime of work in the urban desert of the Southwest.

This book is an unusually well-informed exploration of the history and the potential future of metropolitan Phoenix. We are proud to have had a role in its publication.

John Meunier
Dean, College of Architecture and Environmental Design
Arizona State University

Acknowledgments ━━━━━━━

Lots of people helped produce this book, though none should be blamed for it. My partners at Gammage and Burnham generously allowed me to take six months away from practicing law. Stephen Anderson and Jeff Miller deserve special thanks for explaining to clients with ongoing matters that I had temporarily lost my mind, but their problems would be handled. Crystal Boglio typed early drafts from dictated tapes, trying to make sense of rambling narratives.

The College of Architecture and Environmental Design was a wonderful place to hang out. John Meunier and everyone on the faculty helped me to appreciate life in academia. Fritz Steiner's own sabbatical in Rome opened up an office for me to use, and David Pijawka could not have been more gracious when I shoved all his books into a corner so I could be surrounded by my stuff. Sasha Valdez helped me figure out how to navigate through the bureaucracy of ASU.

At the Herberger Center, working with Mary Kihl and the staff was efficient and enjoyable. Audrey Morris, the editor, was thorough, careful, attentive, and unfailingly professional. A succession of student researchers worked hard to come up with some support for assertions I made. Brenton Elmore did a great job of designing the cover and the initial layouts.

In the larger community, a great many people acted as sounding boards and resources and helped me assemble information. A few of them were: Carol Johnson, Dave Richert, Leslie Dornfeld, Rob Melnick, Mary Jo Waits, John Hall, John F. Long, Alan Maguire, Joel Nilsson, Sid Wilson, Larry Dozier, Reed Kroloff, and Mike Martin. Large numbers of elected officials, city employees, and citizens active in zoning and development decisions have taught me many things over the years, sometimes in late night, high tension meetings. I thank them all.

The most consistently supportive and valuable friend through this process was Debbie Abele, my partner in teaching preservation planning at ASU. She helped locate many of the historic sources in the early chapters, provided valuable editorial comment, covered for me in our class, ran interference with sources, and helped make my life better during this exercise.

Finally, I must especially thank my wife Karen and my sons, Chris, Matt, and Andrew, for putting up with my apparently interminable mid-life crisis, which leads me off into doing things like this book.

Introduction

The little boy in the middle seat wants to climb on top of me to look out the window. As he squirms, his tennis shoes dig into my lap, and together we press our faces to the plastic. There is not much to see-there are no trees or buildings or people, no sign of life at all. From 20,000 feet up, the land is flat, gray, and vast, punctuated by scattered rock piles, some big enough to be mountains. Except for the blue of the sky, we could be looking at an asteroid. Everyone else on the plane seems to know that, since only this kid and I are bothering with more than a glance.

The pitch of the engines changes and the plane begins to descend. Dark dots of creosote are clustered along braided washes, making them look like green varicose veins. Every so often there is the thin straight line of an apparent road, leading from nothing to nowhere. Then suddenly, huge smooth rectangles appear to be sewn into a patchwork with remnant squares of unbladed desert. The grid of human presence means these are farms, but at first there are no barns or houses or lush crops, just flatter land and darker dirt. The plane banks tightly so our view is only sky. Across the cabin the opposite window frames a fragment of civilization: the curvy streets, houses, and yards of Phoenix.

"See," I say to the boy, motioning for him to look to the other side, "people do live here." He moves back into his own seat, as I hoped he would, and I brush off my lap. As the plane levels, the vision from the other window expands toward the horizon. Golf courses, larger buildings, black asphalt, and cars are added to the sea of houses. His mom smiles at me and reaches over to fasten his seatbelt.

Examinations of Phoenix tend to begin in the air. Michael Sorkin, writing in *Architectural Record*, flies in at night, when "inky emptiness abuts the grid of lights, the desert lapping at the edges of town." In *Legends of the American Desert*, Alex Shoumatoff finds himself seated next to a Nebraskan who is on his way to Lake Havasu City to marry off his daughter in the land of London Bridge. When *Newsweek* examined the phenomenon of suburbs in May 1995, it began with an aerial view of Phoenix as a way to capture the boundless sense of space. In *Cadillac Desert*, Marc Reisner looks down on the desert to think about what is missing—water. Flying into Phoenix conveys the isolation of a metropolis that sits improbably as an island in the middle of an inhospitable sea of creosote, cactus, and venomous creatures.[1]

It is tempting, even fashionable, to see Phoenix as some kind of sociological mistake—a giant urban catastrophe in a place that should never have held significant numbers of people in the first place. In the planning jargon of the day, a place that is "unsustainable." Indeed, a recent travel commentary reaches that conclusion, calling Phoenix and Tucson "two of the most ludicrous cities on earth." As if that were not enough, it seems nearly impossible to pick up any newspaper or journal without being reminded what an awful curse "sprawl" is on the American landscape, and that Phoenix is the poster child of the disease. Fast food outlets, office parks, and shopping centers rising out of barren plains of asphalt are said to be the source of widespread civic malaise. Richard Moe sees residential subdivisions spreading like inkblots, creating a graveyard of livability and drowning communities in the destructive, soulless, ugly mess of sprawl. James Howard Kunstler thinks sprawl erodes even our patriotism. As he proclaimed to a Phoenix audience, "No American boy will fight and die for the Burger King."[2]

Many critics of the urban form of places like Phoenix neither live, nor try very hard to understand, the lifestyle they pejoratively term sprawl. Urging a return to the architectural archetypes of an earlier era, they see the automobile and the detached single-family home as the principal villains in the loss of pedestrian scale, the separation of land uses, and the large lots of suburbia that have cut the bonds of city life. Only by radically attempting to alter development patterns, largely in emulation of that longed-for past, do such critics argue that we can create a viable future.[3]

Today, so pervasive and accepted is the criticism of suburban growth patterns that even suburban dwellers have taken up the cry of indictment. *The Arizona Republic*, principal champion of growth in the Valley of the Sun over the last 75 years, ran a series of articles in 1995–96 titled "An Acre an Hour: The Price of Sprawl." By 1998, a crescendo of concern about Phoenix's growth was reflected in nearly daily articles in the local press about growth issues, in publications including the Morrison Institute's *Growth in Arizona: The Machine in the Garden*, and in political debate about the relative virtues of growing smarter or urban growth boundaries. At nearly every Phoenix social gathering—even those populated by developers—concern about growth is evident. "We've just got to do something," accompanied by a furrowed brow, is the usual refrain.

Yet despite all this criticism, Phoenix is perennially one of the fastest growing places in America.[4] In 1997, a year in which homebuilding in the metropolitan area was supposed to cool off, 31,715 single-family permits were issued. The migration of Americans to the south and west has not been halted even by increased urban vitality in the north and east. All over the country, the predominant pattern of living continues to head toward cars and detached homes. Today, more than 80 percent of the people in America live in the suburbs that so many sources attack.

The paradox of the continued growth and success of the very development patterns that are relentlessly criticized cannot be dismissed simply as a conflict between the views of an intellectual elite and the choices of the common man. The tension is evident within individuals living the suburban life. In many ways, the people who live in the new cities of the American Southwest are modern nomads—transplants drawn from somewhere else by the promise of sunshine, affordability, and jobs. Their rootlessness presages a future in which people can live where they want and move when they want, as often as they want. For every five people who move into Phoenix, three move out. Their places of employment are likely in a suburban location, which may or may not be near home. The odds are overwhelming that their house is made of stucco, in some minor variation on the theme of beige, and the roof is red tile. They shop in a big box building surrounded by vast parking lots. Their lifestyle is that of the homogenized American place. But while many contemporary critics find this both tragic and deplorable, the odds are that these suburbanites like their personal existence. They just wish there were not so many other people living the same way, and they blame growth, sprawl, and developers for a deterioration in their lifestyle.

I am one of these conflicted Phoenicians. I love living in Phoenix. I was born here, and my permanent address has always been here. I like my detached single-family home, my backyard, and my cul-de-sac. I like my neighborhood, and most of my neighbors. I like driving my car wherever I want. I like walking out of my house, down the street, and into South Mountain Park, where I can sit on a rock and admire the view. And I refuse to conclude that this place is either ludicrous or unsustainable.

We have done many things well in building Phoenix. Our streets have nicer landscaping than most places in America. We heavily restrict signs, leading to much less visual clutter than most other major metropolitan areas. On average, the quality of our architecture and urban design is relatively high. Our shopping centers are better looking and better landscaped than those you will see in Dallas or Houston or Las Vegas. While we worry that growth does not pay for itself, that growth has ensured the fiscal integrity of our cities, which maintain some of the highest bond ratings in the nation.

Like most people who have lived here for a long time, I appreciate the benefits that attach to our status as a big city—the museums, sports teams, and things to do. I started working in downtown Phoenix in the late 1960s, and it has steadily improved as the city has grown. I grew up in Tempe, and its transformation into an interesting place is testament to the power of an urban vision—as well as the benefits of thousands of pedestrians and the urban diversity of body piercing. But like other long-time Phoenicians, I miss less crowded streets, cleaner air, and cooler nights. And like everyone—newcomers and old-timers—I worry about what we are losing as we develop the desert.

The low-density fabric of the new urban Southwest is far from perfect. Many neighborhoods are bleak garagescapes of identical homes distinguished only by the colors of the cars in the driveway or the shape of the single window facing the street. The great boulevards of the nearly endless grid are often lined with parking lots, separating the citizens of the community from whatever kernels of architecture there may be. Many people do not know their neighbors until they get together to complain about the new development being proposed behind them. So I understand when the neo-traditional critics look at places like Phoenix and blanch. They fear a future that seems to be emerging: a time in which places all run together in a world of Internet connections, chain stores, and asphalt.

This book began when I took a sabbatical from the practice of law to spend six months at the ASU College of Architecture and Environmental Design, beginning in January 1998. I had been teaching classes there and in the College of Law for several years, and had written some previous articles on urban growth issues. Mostly, though, for 20 years I have worked as a zoning lawyer: a messenger of growth and, like the clients I represent, a carrier of the plague called development. Night after night, month after month, I have stood in tense neighborhood meetings trying to communicate basic tenets of the social compact: You moved here and so will others; some will need to live in apartments; some will need to shop at Target. No, the city cannot just tell my client that he is not allowed to build on his property. No, that land behind you was never designated to be open space, even if the broker who sold you your house said so. No, the city cannot mandate that any home near you have a minimum sales price or be occupied only by people just like you. Yes, the streets will get more crowded.[5]

Angry citizens in a zoning hearing are interested neither in learning the history of their city, nor in revisiting high school civics. But failing to recognize the social and political forces that create particular cities makes impossible any useful dialogue about future growth. For those who are interested in these issues beyond dealing with an immediate perceived threat, the intent of this book is to provide some help in elevating the dialogue.

To do that, it is first necessary to understand as best we can why the Valley of the Sun looks the way it does. Part I of this book, Concentration and Dispersal, looks at the forces shaping this urban area. This is not a comprehensive retelling of the history of Phoenix, but rather personal observations on a few of the major factors within that history that have had an especially evident impact on urban form. Chapter 1 deals with the late nineteenth and early twentieth century history of settlement of this desert by a scruffy group of entrepreneurs determined to establish a desirable place to live. Chapter 2 looks at the issue of water, and how it acts as a social and physical binding agent among people in an arid environment. Chapter 3 is concerned with the post-war boom that created a major metropolis based on the mass-produced single-family home. Finally, Chapter 4 examines some of the growing pains evident since 1970.

Part II, Agents So Commonplace, is a snapshot look at the current status of our metropolitan area and the potential changing dynamics of life in the future. First, what about that awful sprawl? Chapter 5 tries to insert some substance into the "down with sprawl" mantra chanted by people living the very lifestyle they indict. Chapter 6 suggests we recognize that we are on the edge of an urban transformation as profound as that wrought by the automobile. Chapter 7 deals with the thorny problem of what limits might ultimately slow our population growth, and how we might use limits as a planning tool.

With his book *Designing the Future*, Vernon Swaback inaugurated the College of Architecture and Environmental Design's book series, The Phoenix Dialogues. Swaback and I share a history of being involved in particular development projects, often ones with attendant controversy. We both come out of those battles convinced that the polarized anger of such individual decisions is seldom productive. Somewhere between those who see developers as demons, and those property owners who believe their rights to exploit that which they own are absolute, there ought to be a balance. Somewhere between believing that growth is an end in itself, and fearing that growth brings the end, there ought to be a way to live in the desert.

Vernon Swaback is an artist, and his challenge was to provide us with thoughts about *Designing the Future*. Lawyer that I am, mine is to think about managing it. Part III, Pieces of a Puzzle, looks at six specific issues within the growth debate and how the process of dealing with these factors might be better managed. These include: open space preservation, single-family home and neighborhood design, state trust land, transportation, paying for the costs of growth, and the development permitting process.

Time to move my seatback to the full upright. I show the kid where the button is so he can do it himself, and he smiles at me. Behind us two guys with southern accents sound distressed as we near Sky Harbor. There still is not enough green to make them comfortable, and they wouldn't want to live in this place. We are now flying over the dry Salt River bed, but they don't know that.

"Look over there," one says, "they sure piled up a whole lot of dirt next to that football stadium. I wonder where they're going to put it."

It's a butte, you idiot, I think to myself.

It feels good to be home.

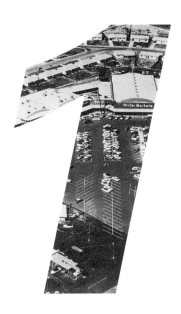

Concentration and Dispersal —————————

Betting on a Boom ━━━━━━━━━━━━━━

When the United States Census Bureau first noted the disappearance of the frontier line, only 20 years had passed since John Wesley Powell floated through the Grand Canyon. As the frontier moved west, it jumped over the desert on its way to the Pacific. In the ensuing years, the "frontier" pressed in on the desert Southwest from both California and the Great Plains.[1]

Frederick Jackson Turner believed the frontier had created a safety valve that allowed America's social development to be continually reborn.[2] The frontier produced in the American character an independence of spirit along with occasional antisocial tendencies and antipathy toward government control. The rugged individualism born of free land sometimes led to selfishness more than civic mindedness.[3] Life on the frontier was life on the margin, where rules and ethical expectations were elastic. In 1890, the City of Phoenix had 3,152 "citizens" marooned in one of the most isolated and inhospitable parts of the country. Those hardy souls who were willing to brave the blistering heat of summer epitomized Turner's vision—individualists without class distinctions, outcasts hoping to reinvent their lives, marginal entrepreneurs in search of economic bonanza, missionaries in the transformative process of settlement, forefathers of a community that would come to see development as a reason to be.

Phoenix's generally accepted modern history began in 1867 when Jack Swilling of Wickenburg realized that the Salt River Valley offered farmland free of rocks and frost. Swilling was a former Confederate soldier and deserter, a Union army freighter and scout, a prospector, a farmer, a speculator, a drunk, and a scoundrel. By March 1868, diverted water from the Salt was flowing in his ditch. Most accounts hold that it was Darrell Duppa, a similarly colorful eastern expatriate banished by his family, who suggested the name Phoenix. He thought it suitable for the new town "springing from the ruins" of the civilization of the Hohokam, who had disappeared around 1450, probably in response to a prolonged drought.

The settlement began largely as a small supply outpost and trading center established to serve Fort McDowell, a military camp located to the northeast. In 1868, about 50 people inhabited Phoenix and cultivated 1,000 acres of irrigated farmland. After the construction of Swilling's ditch, new settlers, farmers, and pioneers poured in and by 1870 a townsite location was sel-ected, a mile north of the Salt River because of occasional floods. As at other urban settlements along the frontier, the founders of Phoenix were largely in search of fortunes they had not made elsewhere.[4] From the outset, Swilling and his partners grew crops and sold land, seeking to profit from the enterprise of settlement. An 1870 survey platted lots: the first sold for $103.[5]

The early Phoenicians worked unceasingly to become connected by railroad to the rest of the nation, believing that such a connection would bring people and goods across the desert to make the oasis boom. A spur line to Maricopa in 1879 formed the beginning of such a link, though the railhead was still a 16-hour wagon ride from Phoenix. Even at that, people could get to the city and agricultural goods could be shipped out. Finally, in 1887, the Southern Pacific extended the spur from Maricopa to Phoenix. The coming of the railroad was one of the bases for the recognition by the legislature that the state capital should be moved to centrally located Phoenix.

The completion of the rail link and the opening of a fire brick factory made conventional building materials more available. Brick and wood structures began to replace adobe in popularity. The city's boosters wanted the buildings of Phoenix to look more "American."[6] Similarly, the settlement was platted in a square-mile grid in 1876. In this, Phoenix followed early American town models where pre-planning of city form was made possible by available land and an expectation of settlement. The grid was especially well suited to flatlands and non-port locations, where the center of town was simply the intersection of two streets. Thomas Jefferson, one of the great architects of American history, was a strong believer in the grid pattern for frontier towns. A classicist, Jefferson had studied the regular geometries of the Greeks and valued the grid because of its efficiency.[7]

The quest to look more like gridded American cities meant looking less like the native urban cultures of the Southwest. In their cliff dwellings, the Anasazi walked directly from roof to roof. Pueblo Grande, a Hohokam village lying within the Phoenix city limits, was a tightly packed village of interlocking houses, rooms, and community structures. These kinds of dwellings made little sense to settlers of European descent, who desired to separate private and public property. The early settlers of Phoenix might have been outcasts or even failures in other parts of America, but it was those places they wanted to replicate. To make their city grow, they needed to attract migrants. City form and housing types, even then, were driven largely by marketing concerns. So they rejected the native building traditions, believing them to be dirty, primitive, and uncivilized.[8]

Throughout its infancy, Phoenix grew steadily but did not boom. Even the completion of the railway spur from Maricopa did not result in the doubling or tripling of property values that had been optimistically predicted. There were still too many impediments to growth. The river was unpredictable, and more irrigation works and storage areas were needed to stabilize the water supply. The protection of the U.S. Army was inconsistent. The initial federal homestead allowance of 160 acres was inadequate for farming in the desert environment.[9] The embryonic Arizona desert city lacked the impetus that the discovery of precious metals brought to Denver, the religious imperative of

Pueblo Grande, the Hohokam's main village in what is now the City of Phoenix.
Pueblo Grande Museum, City of Phoenix

Salt Lake City, or the location of El Paso on a major trade route. So, at the turn of the century, population statistics dramatically reflected these differences: Denver, 134,000; Salt Lake, 53,000; El Paso, 16,000; Phoenix 5,500.

Despite the slow growth, this early era in the Valley's history had begun to establish patterns. Deliberate hard work was necessary to survive in the desert: farming required ingenuity and investment in water systems, and construction required importing materials. There was a willingness to experiment in search of success—there were not a lot of tested formulae on how to live in such a place. It took ingenuity not just to profit, but to figure out how to survive.

As in most American cities, development in Phoenix initially followed the primary transportation route—the streetcar system. The Phoenix Street Railway Company began service in 1887, and by 1892 included eight miles of track running on Washington Street and Central Avenue. At the turn of the century, the lines were extended beyond the city limits, bringing with them an ability to develop new areas. A number of individuals and small investment companies began platting land on the outskirts into subdivisions with lots of about 50 feet by 130 feet. In deference to the local climate, most lots were oriented north/south, to avoid facing houses directly into the morning or afternoon sun.

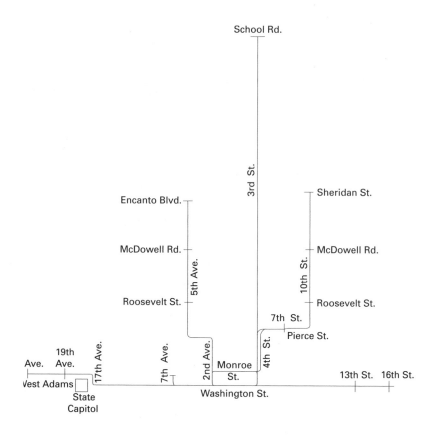

Phoenix's streetcar system in 1938.
Source: Fleming 1977

Just as in Los Angeles, real estate owners and investors, recognizing the value of the streetcar line, were easily convinced to pay the construction costs of extending the rail lines. As a result of streetcar expansion, 16 new subdivisions were platted in the year 1909 alone.[10]

A giant figure in the early history of Phoenix was Dwight B. Heard. Heard moved to Phoenix in 1895, hoping the climate would help him recover his health. With the backing of his rich father-in-law, he purchased a 7,500-acre ranch along the Salt River where he raised cattle and grew alfalfa, cotton, oranges, and grapefruit. He also purchased 160 acres of prime development land on Central Avenue north of McDowell Road. There he developed a prestigious residential subdivision, Los Olivos, where he built his own house, which he opened to guests from the east to whom he sought to sell real estate.

In 1911, Heard began advertising the sale of portions of his ranch in ten- and 40-acre homesteads. In his ads, Heard described city life negatively.

Subsistence farming appealed to his paternalistic notion of being one's own man and becoming economically independent. Heard expanded his influence by taking over less successful subdivisions, using his growing development acumen to market them to new Phoenicians. He bought a subdivision from Frances Q. Story, a Los Angeles investor and citrus farmer who had found it cheaper to speculate on land in Phoenix than in Los Angeles. Story had begun offering homesites in the vicinity of Grand Avenue, but initial interest was low. In 1924, after the completion of Cave Creek Dam, the plat was taken over by Heard's investment company. He paved the streets and completed installation of city sewer service and gas and electric lines throughout the entire 40-acre development.[11]

Heard was an archetype. He wanted Phoenix to boom, both so he could personally profit and because he believed in the city and its future. In this he was typical of a breed lured by Turner's frontier of opportunity. From the late nineteenth century on, that frontier had given rise to the phenomenon of the boomtown, where fortunes were quickly made in speculative real estate. When Tocqueville traveled the American frontier, he passed through a number of boomtowns, giving rise to his observation that "an American changes his residence ceaselessly."[12] These newly built cities were practical contrivances to be started from scratch, built up, and quickly abandoned or altered.[13] Civic leaders in such places were also promoters out for personal profit. Like Heard, they had migrated in search of a better life, and became boosters of the benefits of that life. The attachment of this kind of leader to a place is very different than that of a third-generation Boston Brahmin. The goal is not to maintain or preserve, but to build—to be the agent of positive change brought by growth.

As a result of the efforts of Heard and others, early-twentieth-century Phoenix subdivisions were built with varying lot sizes and bungalow-style houses typical of California. The spiraling real estate market of the Golden State consistently provided inspiration. In 1910, two Phoenix realtors, Greene and Griffin, returned from a conference in California with a scheme to build houses on lots which they platted and then sold as a unit—house and land—on an easy payment plan. Prior to this time, the common practice was to buy a lot, and then contract to have a house built. Packaging lot and home together and offering financing was an innovation that greatly expanded the potential home-buying market. For as little as ten percent down and $25 a month, local residents could become homeowners in Phoenix's newest and most desirable neighborhoods.

Greene and Griffin went on to establish Homebuilders, Inc., a company that continued to be an innovator in the housing market. The company built in different parts of town and in different market segments, constantly experimenting in search of a winning formula for building Phoenix.

The fact that the boom did not occur too easily or too quickly gave impetus to this climate of experimentation. There was no established method of construction or style that defined the Arizona house. Different styles could be adapted and tested for acceptance.

Private automobiles arrived in Phoenix in the summer of 1900. The automobile was an instant hit in the Southwest. The hard flat soil meant that cars were useful even without paved roads. By 1910 there were 382 licensed cars in Phoenix and an automobile club was lobbying for roads to other Arizona cities. A special committee (led by Heard) visited Los Angeles, El Paso, and other cities to study street pavement. When they returned, 19 blocks of the business core were paved based on their recommendations. In 1920, a local official said, "The people in this town have forgotten how to walk, if they have to go two blocks, they get in a machine and drive." Reflecting this growing attachment to motor travel, the number of cars registered in the county rose from 646 in 1913, to 11,539 in 1920, to 53,064 in 1929.[14]

Streetcars had allowed cities to spread out along linear spokes, and filling in between the spokes was limited by how far residents could comfortably walk. Cars broke this pattern, and in Phoenix, as in Los Angeles, the car actually led to what we today might call infill development. New real estate was opened up for development as a result, and the city form changed from a hub with spokes to an ever-expanding grid of blocks linked by asphalt. New subdivisions served only by the automobile were beginning to dominate the growth pattern of most western cities by the 1920s.[15]

The onset of World War I brought a slowing in the population growth of Phoenix. The effect of this slowdown was offset by a dramatic increase in the demand for agricultural products. Long-staple cotton was essential to the war effort because it was used in manufacturing tires, balloons, and airplane fabric. The climate of the Valley, with its year-round growing season, is ideal for cotton production. By 1918, cotton replaced alfalfa as the area's leading crop. Widespread demand saw the price of cotton soar from 28¢ to $1.35 a pound during the war years. As a result, land suited to cotton production similarly escalated in price from $60 to as high as $500 an acre.[16]

In 1924, the Southern Pacific began leasing the El Paso and Southwest Railway, linking El Paso to Los Angeles, with Phoenix the largest city in between. Additional reclamation projects on the Salt River improved irrigation and enabled the citrus and cattle industries to expand. In 1920, Phoenix passed Tucson to become the largest city in the state and by 1930 was the second largest city in the Southwest with a population of 48,000. El Paso dominated the region with 102,000.

The idea that cities should develop in an orderly, planned, and regulated fashion became prominent in the 1920s with the advent of zoning ordinances. Comprehensive zoning began in 1916 as an attempt to reduce crowding and bring light and air to the tenements of New York City, and to separate industrial uses from residences. In the early 1920s, the U.S. Department of Commerce published a model state zoning enabling act to encourage the use of zoning ordinances as a means of guiding community development. Ultimately, the act was adopted by all 50 states, and after the U.S. Supreme Court validated zoning as a constitutional use of the police power in 1926, zoning ordinances multiplied across the country.[17] All these early ordinances evidenced the prevalent attitude that the purpose of zoning was to protect neighborhoods of single-family houses from other, more noxious, land uses.

Throughout the growing Southwest and southern California, zoning was quickly seized upon by real estate entrepreneurs as a means of stabilizing property values by ensuring that entire areas would develop consistently. Zoning became a tool to limit undesirable uses and populations to certain parts of town. Previously, the only control available was through deed restrictions imposed on land by the owner. Using zoning, developers could extend their vision of a consistent homogeneous community onto their neighbors' property.

In Phoenix, the first serious experiment with city planning began in 1920 when the city retained a Chicago firm to develop a plan for land use, roadways, and park sites.[18] The plan exemplified the City Beautiful movement, proposing a physical design for the community complete with broad boulevards and classical buildings. Pursuant to the proposals, the Phoenix Planning Commission was created to develop a general plan. The new commission, headed by William Hartranft, began to press for a city zoning ordinance. Hartranft was not only chair of the commission, he was also the "father of Phoenix parks," a cement products manufacturer, and a developer of the Kenilworth, Palmcroft, and Chelsea Place subdivisions. In 1926, he wrote a series of articles for *The Arizona Republican* extolling the virtues of zoning relative to property values and real estate marketing. He also appealed to competitive instincts, noting that few cities of Phoenix's size lacked zoning, and that 47 cities in California had zoning but in Arizona there was only one—Chandler. Since Phoenix was "competing" for the same "class of citizens" as California, it needed zoning. In 1930 the city adopted a comprehensive zoning ordinance.

While zoning was beginning to take hold as a factor in ordering land use and city growth in Phoenix, homebuilding was evolving as an industry. Due to fierce competition among the segments of the development community, innovation became a major determinant of success. With vacillations between periods of high demand with no available housing stock and building gluts in the face of poor economic times and waning population growth, the successful entrepreneur was one who stayed in tune with and even ahead of subtle changes in the marketplace.

During the 1920s, the development pattern began to move beyond simple preparation of lots to marketing, promotion, and delivery of finished homes. Many methods were used to help a potential buyer select a home. One of the most common was the plan book, which offered a variety of standardized house layouts and a catalog of features that could be added to customize the plan. Newspaper advertising provided picturesque renderings of what a house might look like, but such ads were still two-dimensional in form. Building a house on speculation was a more effective marketing tool, allowing potential buyers the possibility of viewing their prospective investment in all its splendor.

The use of model homes is an example of the type of innovation that began to change the industry. Model homes were used to illustrate the character and style of different housing alternatives. This worked especially well for the Period Revival homes of the 1920s. Subdivisions might have Colonial and Mediterranean style houses mixed with Tudor and more traditional forms. The fervor for Period Revival was a national movement related to increased pride in the nation's heritage after World War I. Nationally, Colonial Revival was most prominent, but, in Phoenix, Spanish Colonial Revival, Mediterranean, and Pueblo Revival tended to predominate.[19] Architects created models based on these different styles and a buyer might see Tudor, Spanish, and Pueblo Revival examples of a single floor plan. New subdivisions also featured infrastructure amenities to give an area character and define its position among competing new developments. Heard and Hartranft's Palmcroft subdivision, for example, featured evenly spaced California fan palms along the curvilinear City Beautiful streets. The streets' circular pattern was designed to focus traffic to the interior of the subdivision rather than along the connector streets between the major avenues.

The evolution of Phoenix homebuilders from contractors of individual houses to developers came as early as the 1920s. This phenomenon is generally thought to have originated largely in California, though most development in Los Angeles continued to separate homebuilding from lot development until well into the 1930s.[20] However, by 1927 several builder-driven subdivisions existed in Phoenix.

The transition from single lot sales into actual home construction was simple economics. A subdivider who obtains plat approval and installs streets and utilities is called in industry jargon a "horizontal developer." This type of work is capital intensive but not labor intensive. Early in the century it came to be dominated, therefore, by bankers, realtors, and businessmen. A horizontal developer assumes the costs of owning the land and the expense of

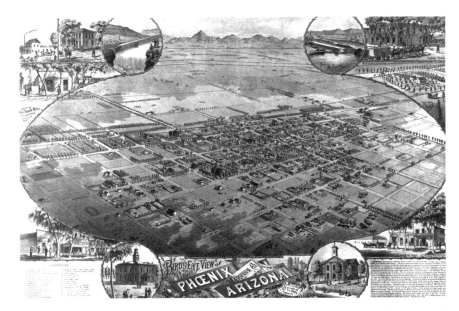

Phoenix's grid pattern is clearly visible in this early bird's-eye view, looking to the northeast.
The Arizona Historical Society—Central Arizona Division

constructing streets and infrastructure.[21] He hopes to sell lots to homebuilders (or "vertical developers") as quickly as possible to recoup his large up-front costs. Homebuilders were often undercapitalized tradesmen-carpenters and masons who built a few houses each year. In order to get an undercapitalized vertical builder to buy the lots, the horizontal developer had to offer a number of concessions, such as a very low down payment and no carrying costs for several months, in order to allow the homebuilder time to find buyers for his houses. The homebuilder's financial commitment was thereby limited, but the land developer was incurring an increasing level of obligation with no cash flow—in effect, subsidizing the individual homebuilder. It was a natural economic move for the lot developers to move into the homebuilding business, integrating the horizontal and vertical components of the residential development process.

Coincident with the rise of the homebuilder-developer in Phoenix was a growing concern at the federal level that there was a crisis in American homeownership. Between 1890 and 1930, the proportion of Americans who owned their own homes had risen from 36 percent to 47 percent. But the depression reversed the trend, and by 1940, only 41 percent were homeowners.[22] This small change was viewed as the beginning of an alarming trend reversing decades of progress. As a result, under the Coolidge administration,

Secretary of Commerce Herbert Hoover was made chairman of the Better Homes in America Commission. Coolidge explained the need for such a movement: "The American home is the foundation of our national and individual well being."[23] The involvement of the federal government in single-family homebuilding in America had begun.

Writing for *Fortune* magazine in 1932, Archibald MacLeish characterized homebuilding in the United States as an industry the industrial revolution had passed by.[24] The magazine expressed a direct interest in increasing the size of homebuilding companies in order to achieve the economies of scale that had benefited other industries. The federal interest in homebuilding further mushroomed in the face of the Great Depression. What began as a growing concern became a national imperative to improve the country's living conditions. In 1931, the President's Conference on Home Building and Home Ownership set the framework for many of the New Deal policies: replacement of short-term mortgages with the long-term amortized mortgage, federally backed loans, and the reduction of homebuilding costs through large-scale residential development and standardized building practices. By absolutely asserting a new American truth—that ownership of the detached single-family home was an American birthright to which all citizens could aspire—these policies became the most influential set of government actions ever to affect the space and character of American cities.

The Federal Housing Administration (FHA) was established in 1934 as a permanent federal agency, taking over the work of the Better Homes in America Commission. Employing tradesmen and stabilizing the country's lending environment became just as important as increasing home ownership. Since the FHA would insure mortgages, the agency developed requirements for acceptable home construction standards, neighborhood plans, and even suitable locations, all to help protect its guarantees. In an effort to address the perceived deficiencies in home ownership and in homebuilding as an industry, the FHA undertook a "scientific search for the minimum size house."[25] The goal was to standardize the production of houses in order to lower cost and increase the number of homeowners, just as Henry Ford did for automobiles. Basements and attics were criticized as needless wastes of space. In 1936, the FHA came out with a minimum house prototype of 624 square feet. The search for "safe" locations led the FHA to prefer new, uniform, standardized subdivisions. It also led to widespread government-sanctioned emphasis on neighborhood racial homogeneity as further evidence of stability.

Ultimately, federal involvement in homebuilding dramatically increased the percentage of American homeowners. These policies spurred more efficient construction techniques, as had been hoped. But the climate of experimentation in homebuilding that had characterized earlier periods would begin to change. With government oversight, construction experimentation—especially to reduce cost—was encouraged. Design experimentation was not.

In contrast to most of America, the Great Depression did not devastate Arizona. Phoenix continued to develop. Arizona received more money per capita from federal programs than did most states, a result of strong local leadership from the business and civic communities. Early on, Walter Bimson and Valley National Bank were especially important in realizing how to take advantage of the New Deal programs. Another local business leader, Del Webb, quickly found ways to use New Deal programs to put people to work. Webb had started work in Phoenix as a carpenter in the 1920s and began his own construction firm in the early 1930s. New Deal grants and loans enabled Webb and other contractors to reap millions of dollars for building projects throughout the Valley. At the end of the 1930s, Webb himself stated, "Construction is no longer a private enterprise, but rather a subsidiary of the federal government."[26]

The national thrust for single-family homebuilding played well with the civic boosters of Phoenix, who were still seeking to put their city on the map. This was especially evident in the pages of *The Arizona Republican*, which featured each new subdivision opening during the 1930s as proof positive of the increasing sophistication of the city. Just as today, developers of these early subdivisions sought to promote their projects as "residential communities" with a desirable character and lifestyle.

By 1940, most of the key ingredients for Phoenix to grow were in place. The flat farmland of the Salt River Valley could be subdivided and built on as easily as it could be plowed for cotton and citrus farming. The year-round growing season could also support continuous construction. The ubiquitous grid of streets was easily extended so the auto could provide access to each new piece of the checkerboard. A successful local industry based upon integrated development of land and construction was well positioned to take advantage of a hoped-for surge in homebuilding. Phoenix's emergence as the state capital further diversified the economy beyond agriculture. Although rarely acknowledged, the quiet reliance on federal government programs and dollars also had meant that the city fared relatively well in the depression.

Perhaps most importantly, the community leadership believed strongly in the potential for growth. That leadership consisted of people who cared about their city and would personally prosper from its development. Through planning and zoning, local government could protect against the perceived negatives of development and stabilize single-family neighborhoods and property values. Those were highly desirable results that served to encourage further growth.

But the longed-for big boom still did not occur. Despite the best efforts of Phoenix boosters, the city continued a pattern of steady but relatively slow growth. At the end of 1940, Maricopa County had more people than El Paso County and was the most populous area in the Southwest. However, Phoenix itself was still at 65,000 people to El Paso's 100,000.[27] Salt Lake had reached 150,000, and Denver had nearly 325,000.

As entrepreneurs, the Phoenicians in the first part of the century hoped that the combination of sunshine and cheap land would attract large numbers of new citizens. They had come to view real estate profit itself as the motivating force for growth. The realization that development could be an industry all on its own came to Phoenix at about the same time it was recognized in Los Angeles. This notion was something new to city building: a future driven not by migration to employment locations, but rather by developers motivated by profit who would seek out both employers and residents.[28] Between 1900 and 1930, Los Angeles literally exploded from this formula, growing by a factor of ten. But having the vision was not the same thing as achieving it. Los Angeles had attractions Phoenix lacked: temperate summers, an ocean, the Rose Parade. Phoenix, on the other hand, was still too dry, too hot, and too thorny. To most Americans, the desert Southwest remained a foreign and inhospitable place, useful as a movie set and a refuge for eccentrics, but not as a place to live. To change that view would require time, technology, and one more generation of boosters.

Liquid Glue ━━━━━━━━━━━

The last time one state brandished arms against another was 1934. The issue was water. Arizona Governor B. B. Moeur dispatched his executive assistant and 102 members of the Arizona National Guard to a God-forsaken spot on the Arizona side of the Colorado River south of Parker. Armed with machine guns, rifles, and tear gas bombs, their mission was to dislodge four one-inch-thick cables that California had connected to the Arizona side to begin the construction of Parker Dam. The dam would divert water from the river into the proposed California Aqueduct, which would carry water to cities served by the Metropolitan Water District. The Arizona troops commandeered two ferryboats. Before the troops could board them, Secretary of the Interior Harold Ickes suspended the dam's construction in the face of the threat and Moeur recalled the troops. The whole affair was written up on the *Los Angeles Times* as the hilarious misadventures of the Arizona Navy. In Arizona, the governor's actions were heralded as the latest in a long line of attempts by Arizona to protect itself against the "greedy paw of the California Bear."[1] In subsequent litigation, Arizona won a ruling that the dam was illegal because it had not been specifically authorized by Congress. Four months later California's congressional delegation fixed that problem and Arizona was left without recourse, "unless it wanted to declare war on the United States."[2]

Among the factors of urban growth in the Southwest, water is the most storied, the most litigated, the most complex. To grow food and sustain human life, three basic ingredients are necessary: sun, water, and land. Of these, only water is portable. In central Arizona, this fact was first recognized by the Hohokam, who built an elaborate irrigation system that provided water to hundreds of thousands of acres by the year 1415. Hohokam settlements tended to be at weak points in the canal systems, where the need to frequently repair breaks made it sensible for people to concentrate. Spanish settlement in New Mexico likewise congregated around water systems. There, the acequia district is the oldest form of government. Acequia is a word of Arabic origin, describing the small dirt and stone ditches that deliver river water to truck farmers and individual property owners. Even today, a thousand old Spanish and Mexican acequia districts are still apportioning water.[3]

An irony of living in the West, a culture purportedly the product of "rugged individualism," is that the need to find water leads to cooperative behavior in settlement building. The coming together of people who benefit from water distributed through ditches is the Southwestern equivalent of a New England town meeting: a cause for celebration of connections. A single farmer, individual, or family seldom has sufficient resources to develop and transport the large amounts of water necessary to sustain agricultural use.

Cooperation among settlers is required, so the earliest forms of government in arid regions tend to be those that deal with water: the acequia, the water district, Jack Swilling and his ditch company.

At some point, an entire settlement's cooperation is insufficient to deal with the water needs. "Outsiders" must be asked to assist in the efforts. In Phoenix, this first occurred in 1883 when William J. Murphy, a railroad contractor, was hired to begin work on the Arizona Canal—this large canal was planned to run through lands the Hohokam had never irrigated on the northern edge of the Valley.[4] But the "outsider" most important to Phoenix was the United States government.

Early on, John Wesley Powell recognized the need for the federal government to play a major role in Western water issues. As one of the first Americans to explore the Grand Canyon, the head of the Smithsonian's Bureau of Ethnology and the U.S. Geological Survey, and the principal author of *Report on the Lands of the Arid Region*, he became the father of Western reclamation. Powell proposed to close the public domain to the spotty settlement that was taking place and instead organize vast areas of the West along geographic lines following hydrological basins within which all of the natural resources would be tied together by the controlling element of water.[5] Water would form the basis for planning Western growth and settlement. First, the federal government would survey the West for the location of irrigable acres and dam sites. Second, homestead allotments would be based on topography, rather than the rectangular grid that had worked so well on the prairies. Farms would be larger and irregular to give everyone water frontage and some irrigable land. Third, since individual initiative and labor were inadequate to develop irrigation works, Powell proposed leaving the control of pasturage lands to cooperative unions—the sort of community commons, or ejido, that had existed in the Spanish villages of New Mexico.

The West of the 1880s was already too settled for Powell's sweeping vision to be accepted. Most settlement had begun, like Phoenix, on the basis of immediate proximity to water. But when the local supply proved inadequate, existing investments in land made it preferable to search for new water sources rather than to move. Instead of a grand scheme to manage hydrologic basins and plan development accordingly, water was a commodity that entrepreneurs sought to move to where they had already established a toehold. Powell only succeeded in convincing Congress to fund an irrigation survey and close the issuance of land patents after 1888. During the first half of the 1890s, John Wesley Powell's grand vision for Western settlement died. Instead of living where water made habitation sensible, water would be moved to wherever people settled.

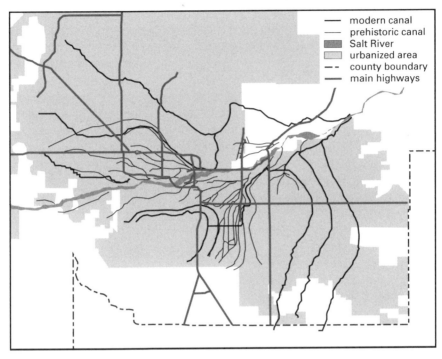

Prehistoric and modern canals in the metropolitan Phoenix area.
Source: Salt River Project

Local realization of the need for cooperative efforts and outside assistance in managing water supplies often came after a crisis of unavailability. Historian Wallace Stegner dates the breakthrough to Congress's funding a geological survey to locate dam sites to the harsh winter of 1886, to the severe droughts of 1887–89, and to the Johnstown Flood. In the case of Phoenix, a similar juxtaposition of maladies did the trick. The droughts of 1898 and 1899 forced a third of the Valley's 200,000 acres of irrigated farmland out of cultivation; a flood in 1890 burst the Walnut Grove Dam on the Hassayampa River, killing 60 people or more; water reached downtown Phoenix in an 1891 flood.[6]

Modern Arizona's reliance on great water projects dates to these events at the turn of the twentieth century. The initial settlers had seen a vision in the remains of the prehistoric canal system and had begun their reconstruction to take advantage of the agricultural potential of the area. Initially, their canals simply diverted flow directly from the Salt River as it went through town—an unreliable method. The early history of constructing those canals is a tale of intrigue, fraud, dishonesty, and armed conflict. When a group of entrepreneurs in one part of the Salt River Valley would band together to construct and operate a canal, they would constantly run into conflict with other past and future operators. The right to water was often transferred with shares in the canal company, rather than with the land being irrigated. The situation was a mess of conflicting priorities and shady legal claims for far more water than actually existed.[7]

In this environment, Arizona territorial representatives and many large landowners, such as Dwight Heard, began pressing local officials and national representatives for major water projects in the West.[8] Benjamin Fowler, a health seeker who moved to Arizona for the climate, became a local advocate of central Arizona as the first major demonstration project of national water reclamation policy. In the fall of 1900, he befriended George Maxwell, Director of the National Irrigation Association, who believed that reclamation of the arid lands of the West would solve the nation's social problems by decentralizing population from urban centers into a vast area that could be developed in accord with Jefferson's agrarian ideal.[9]

When passed in 1902, the Newlands Reclamation Act established the Reclamation Service and authorized a variety of water projects throughout the West—it represents the only major element of Powell's vision that was ever implemented. Users of such projects were required to form cooperative associations to manage the water systems that were constructed and eventually to pay for improvements financed by the federal government. The Salt River Valley Water Users Association (SRVWUA) was formed immediately and in 1903 succeeded in obtaining the authorization for Roosevelt Dam, 60 miles from Phoenix at the confluence of Tonto Creek and the Salt River. In June 1904, the SRVWUA negotiated a contract promising to repay the federal government the cost of building the dam. The members of the association pledged their land as collateral for the repayment of the federal construction loan.[10]

Upon its completion, Roosevelt Dam was the largest masonry dam in the world and created what was then the largest artificial lake in the world. The Salt River Project (SRP) was the first multipurpose reclamation project in the country in that it provided hydroelectric power, delivered water, and gave flood protection to Phoenix. When former President Roosevelt dedicated the dam named after him in 1911, he predicted that central Arizona would become "one of the richest agricultural areas in the world."[11]

In the years following the completion of Roosevelt Dam, the SRVWUA continued to grow and prosper. By 1917, the organization was strong enough to satisfy the federal government that it could operate Roosevelt Dam. The United States continued to hold title to the dam, but the SRVWUA would decide when the water was to be released, how the reservoir was to be operated, and, incidentally, how to deal with the generated electricity. The SRVWUA was controlled by the farmers who had pledged their lands as security, based on a scheme of one vote for each acre of land within the boundary of the irrigated area. In the following years, the federal government built a series of additional dams on both the Salt River and a tributary, the Verde River. Each new dam created another major reservoir providing further stabilization of the water supply, flood control, recreation benefits, and more hydroelectric generating capacity. Eventually the system was able to provide reliable water to over 200,000 irrigated acres, an agricultural empire even larger than that of the Hohokam.

When the Salt River Valley began to urbanize, formerly irrigated agricultural fields became subdivisions. Prior to 1948, only 22,000 acres of farmland had been subdivided, but in the following decade another 32,000 were developed.[12] In most cases, these new urbanizing areas used less water than had the previous agricultural uses, so the conversion did not strain the water systems. As farms turned into neighborhoods, SRP's water was often delivered to individual houses for landscaping that included small citrus orchards.[13] In Tempe, Mesa, and parts of Phoenix, lots still have berms built around them and floodgates in the front yards. Every 10 to 14 days in the summer, the yards are flooded with six inches of water delivered by SRP. Beginning in the early 1950s, following a historic agreement with the City of Phoenix, SRP water began to be delivered to the household tap.

As the Valley grew, SRP added to its electric generating capacity. What had begun as an ancillary benefit of the dams quickly became a major economic engine. In 1937, the state legislature provided for the creation of the Salt River Agricultural Improvement and Power District (this part became known within SRP as "the District") as a municipal subdivision of the state.[14] This permitted SRP to issue municipal bonds to finance construction of coal-fired generating plants to produce more electricity. By the 1990s, power operations had become the major business activity of SRP, producing more than 99 percent of its annual revenues.[15]

Over the years, SRP has successfully cultivated a public image as a beneficial "shadow government" delivering public resources of water and power and managing a vast watershed for the benefit of the Phoenix metropolitan area, even though its somewhat byzantine one acre/one vote system allows its governing boards to continue to be dominated by agricultural interests.[16] This will eventually change with the continued development of land within the SRP boundary. By 2025 the area lying within the boundary of the SRP's original agricultural area will likely be urbanized.[17]

The Salt River Project, which grew out of the complex capital-intensive requirements of handling water in the desert, has given Phoenix stable electric rates, a benign and at times enlightened shadow government, and the water supply needed to safely sustain a huge oasis. SRP is an example of the regional cooperation necessary to manage water in an arid place; it is the direct extrapolation of the tradition of collectivism represented in the acequia.

Even prior to Governor Moeur and the "Arizona Navy," generations of Arizona politicians had made Arizona's right to waters from the Colorado River an article of faith never to be questioned. Once the Salt River had been harnessed, there was nowhere else to turn. To continue to grow both cities and crops, additional water was necessary, and the quest became a recognized community goal. One of the most prominent supporters was George W. P. Hunt, a four-time governor who ignited controversy over the Colorado River virtually every time he mounted a campaign. Hunt believed that Arizona was entitled to the biggest piece of the Colorado's water because the river flows through or is adjacent to the state for almost half of its length, and is fed by a number of tributaries flowing from Arizona. California, by contrast, contributes very little water to the flow of the Colorado. However, it has had a strong claim based on a historic pattern of agricultural use in the Imperial Valley and a large population with great political power.

In 1922, the U.S. Supreme Court ruled that the State of Colorado could not assert the right to all of the water arising within its boundaries, which made the division of its waters among the seven basin states and Mexico legally possible.[18] This would be accomplished by building the largest dam the world had ever seen in Boulder Canyon. The apportionment of the water was set by the signing of the Colorado River Compact in Sante Fe on November 25, 1922. The compact divided the water annually available to the lower basin: 4.4 million acre-feet to California; 2.8 million acre-feet to Arizona; 300,000 acre-feet to Nevada.[19] Governor Hunt opposed ratification of the compact by Arizona, and managed to stampede most of the local residents into believing that it was another plot to steal water from Arizona. Arizona Senators Carl Hayden and Henry Fountain Ashurst joined the fight with a filibuster, but the Boulder Canyon Project Act eventually passed in December 1928. The great dam would be built without Arizona's consent.

Although Arizona refused to ratify the Colorado River Compact for decades, the state finally came to the realization that it was better to fight for federal help to build the necessary works to use the water it had been allocated rather than to assert its claims for more.[20] As a result, the state finally passed the compact in 1944. The hope of providing Colorado River water to Phoenix and central Arizona went back to the turn of the century, using a waterway called the Highline Canal. Fred Coulter, a politician and rancher, had kept the dream of its construction alive through the 1920s and 1930s in public meetings and as part of his repeated runs for governor.

Throughout this period, California continued to draw as much water from the river as it possibly could. In 1952, Los Angeles began planning a second aqueduct and its diversion demands climbed toward more than five million acre-feet—well in excess of its entitlement. In desperation, Arizona filed a case in the U.S. Supreme Court, *Arizona v. California*.[21] After years of litigating, Arizona's lead attorney, Mark Wilmer, realized that the state's best position was actually based on the long-hated Colorado River Compact and Boulder Canyon Project Act. He argued that the water controlled by SRP should not be deducted from Arizona's Colorado River share of 2.8 million acre-feet, and the Supreme Court eventually agreed.

In January 1963 Floyd Dominy, legendary head of the U.S. Bureau of Reclamation, together with Secretary of the Interior and Arizonan Stewart Udall, announced the biggest water project ever: pumping Colorado River water out of Lake Havasu to central Arizona. To produce the electricity to run the massive pumps needed to move the water from Lake Havasu to Phoenix, new dams would be built in Bridge Canyon and Marble Canyon, very close to the Grand Canyon. In one of the earliest and most important victories for the environmental movement, the Sierra Club rallied opposition to the two dams. In response to the Bureau of Reclamation's argument that the reservoirs behind the two dams would make it easier for millions of people to see the Grand Canyon's natural splendor, the club ran one of the most brilliant printed advertisements in American history: "Should we also flood the Sistine Chapel so tourists can get nearer to the ceiling?"[22]

Ultimately, Secretary Udall killed both of the dams and announced a scaled-down Central Arizona Project (CAP). The source of electricity for the project's huge pumps would be a coal-fired power plant already being planned. In 1968, the CAP authorization was signed by President Johnson.[23] To Arizona, the price of this legislation was high: California got its full 4.4 million acre-feet allocation guaranteed as a priority, a right that is senior to Arizona's.[24]

When Jimmy Carter was elected president in 1976, one of his earliest actions was to release a list of Western water projects that he proposed to cut. CAP, by that time, was about half built but on the hit list. Carter failed to understand the religion that is Western water, and there was an immediate bipartisan Western firestorm. As a result, Congress passed most of the capital projects, including the CAP.[25] However, Secretary of the Interior Cecil Andrus exacted a price from the Arizona delegation in exchange for continued CAP funding. Since the state was seriously depleting its groundwater resources, the CAP would only be funded if the state passed pumping limitations. Some suggest that Governor Bruce Babbitt actually engineered the pressure from Secretary Andrus. In response, Babbitt quickly convened a working group of statewide water interests to come up with the 1980

Housing tracts abut the CAP canal in north Phoenix.
Todd Photographic Services

Groundwater Management Act (GMA), one of the most sweeping pieces of legislation in Arizona history.

When the GMA passed, Arizona was consuming about 4.8 million acre-feet of water a year—twice the annual renewable supply. In 1985, farmers still used 89 percent of Arizona's water, yet accounted for only 2 percent of its personal income, while cities used 7 percent of the water and produced 95 percent of the income. By reducing the amount of water consumed by agriculture, most if not all of the groundwater depletion would be eliminated while the urban areas could continue to expand.[26]

The GMA meant a new role for the state in administering Arizona's water resources. The Department of Water Resources (DWR) was created to oversee the administration of the Active Management Areas (AMA) and to issue certificates ensuring a 100-year water supply for subdivisions before land could be sold. In practice, this would force most new development in metropolitan areas to be annexed into existing municipalities. The GMA also required conservation measures for each city in an AMA to reach per capita water use goals.

The GMA is Arizona's most extensive foray into the business of growth management. In the arid West, the dialogue about urban water has not been about quality of life, long-range growth, or development form. The tribal imperative is too strong: we need all the water we can get and we will do anything we can to fight anyone who challenges that assumption. While one group of city dwellers may argue about growth boundaries, population density, and long-term plans, another group—usually engineers and managers—is set on the holy quest for more water. The GMA represented a shift in orientation. Its passage recognized that water should be treated as a resource to be managed—even by controlling growth, if necessary.

At the time the GMA was being negotiated and the DWR being formed, the Bureau of Reclamation continued building the CAP canal. In 1993, Bruce Babbitt, who had become Secretary of the Interior, issued a notice of completion for the five billion dollar ditch, one of the largest public works projects in American history. A series of problems followed. First, the projected demand for the water did not develop. The original contract with the federal government had been based on the assumption that until Arizona's cities needed the full entitlement of water from the Colorado River, farmers would use all they could get. But the canal had grown so expensive that the cost of the water was too high for most agricultural uses.[27] The second problem was that the United States and the Central Arizona Water Conservation District (CAWCD), the state entity created to run the canal and pay back a share of its cost, could not agree on how much the state should pay.[28] Lastly, when the City of Tucson, the CAP's largest municipal customer, starting taking delivery of the water, it came out of the taps a reddish brown color. Although the water was not the problem, this ultimately caused the Tucson voters to shut off their CAP supply and mothball their expensive treatment plant.[29] In part, the opposition to CAP water use was fueled by no-growth sentiments. Some citizens hoped the perception of a crisis would stop development.

These problems meant that, even in the late 1990s, the State of Arizona was still not making full use of its Colorado River allocation. In 1994 the CAP canal, which could deliver up to 1.5 million acre-feet on an annual average, carried about half its capacity.[30] All of Arizona's allocation that went unused was consumed by California. In response to California's thirst, and to ensure sufficient demand to pay for CAP, Arizona began a vigorous campaign to recharge the underground water supply of central Arizona. This meant pumping the water 250 to 300 miles, up more than 2,000 vertical feet, through a fully lined concrete canal, to then dump it into shallow earth basins so that it could drip back into the water table. A series of mechanisms, including the Arizona Water Banking Authority, were created to effect this result. Aquifers which had been depleted over generations are in this way being refilled, while the water is kept away from California.[31]

The final problem confronting CAP was a shift in the attitude of the United States toward reclamation. Originally, the federal government had ventured into the water business as part of a policy to encourage settlement of the West. However, by the time CAP was finally finished, federal reclamation activities had dwindling political support: subsidies for agriculture were no longer viewed as appropriate, and environmental issues had continued to grow in importance. The federal government also had new priorities to resolve long-standing claims to Western water by Indian tribes. When the government sought to use 200,000 or more acre-feet of CAP water to facilitate such settlements with Arizona tribes, local cities and agricultural users protested loudly. "It's our birthright," one city representative said, asserting the claims of his city of snowbirds and transplants against that of the Indians.[32]

The lesson learned from the attempt to use CAP water to settle Indian claims was a reinforcement of the first rule of water in the desert: you can never have enough. Because water's absence is the defining characteristic of a desert, its management becomes the defining activity of living in the desert. The thirst for water supplies has been the initial organizing force for most major desert communities, including Phoenix. Having banded together to fight for water resources, acquisition of that resource becomes the continuing unifying ethic—the most unquestionable goal of government. Controlling water and agreeing to share it defines "us." Others become "them."

The second reality of water in the desert is that delivery is the central problem. The infrastructure cost to develop water is very high and, as a result, "from plumbing flows policy." Only major government action, usually by the federal government, makes it possible to absorb such costs. The plumbing necessary to deliver water in support of people means that development in the desert is a phenomenon of concentration. A desert dweller cannot simply settle wherever he wants, drill a shallow and cheap well, and set up a subsistence farm. He needs access to community systems.

John Wesley Powell's vision of centralized planning, controlled settlement, and community-held assets was too collective and too socialistic to be accepted. To implement Powell's plan would have meant concluding that most of the arid West would never be suitable for habitation. Making such discriminatory judgments at a government level was not a popular thing then, as it would not be popular now. But the failure to plan the growth of the arid West around such restrictions has meant instead that it is structured around the giant plumbing systems that move, concentrate, and redistribute water over vast distances. The economic realities of building such systems has had profound impacts on urban form.

Water development costs lend order to the development of a city in the desert—building can occur only where it can be connected to a source of supply. The result is that desert cities tend to exist in concentrated isolation—wholly unlike the pattern of widely spread towns, farms, and small settlements in the midwest or east. Leapfrog development generally cannot leap very far in a desert environment.[33] There are few truly rural areas on the borders of a desert city. Even farming in the desert is a phenomenon of concentration: both economically, in the hands of large commercial interests which can manage delivery systems; and also geographically, in areas where watercourses are built. Reliance on water delivered through major infrastructure has confined the area of settlement in which people can live to a defined geographic area. In central Arizona, the bubble of urbanization is big, but its outline is distinct. Urban settlement either runs right up to vacant desert, as in north Scottsdale, Las Vegas, or Tucson; or, as on the west side of Phoenix or in the East Valley, there may be a mile or two of farmland acting as a buffer between the urban edge and the desert. The GMA further reinforces this concentration, for today in an AMA no one can simply go 20 miles outside municipal boundaries and drill a new well.

The quest for water gave Phoenix a unifying purpose. Today the question is not how to get more water, but how to manage existing supplies. Yet, other than the single important example of the GMA, water has not been used as a tool to plan among competing uses, to define future growth, or to make decisions about the appropriateness of particular land uses or development patterns. Rather, water management has been treated as a cultural necessity. As a result, the role of water in defining the form of Phoenix has been unintentional and largely unexamined. It has acted as a gravitational pull on residents, forcing together individualists who might otherwise repel one another; pulling them into cooperative and concentrated settlement in a relatively defined area; making a frontier into something resembling a city.

The Industry of Growth ▬▬▬▬▬▬▬▬

Wars transform cities. The instrument of such transformation may be cataclysmic destruction and rebirth; it may be an economic change like the unprecedented bureaucratic buildup in Washington, D.C., in the 1940s; or it may be the result of technological advances. World War II transformed Phoenix through air travel and air conditioning.

Despite the efforts of its leading citizens, Phoenix's rail link to the rest of the country never turned the city into a major transportation hub. Commercial air travel had a different result. Lodged inside a silver fuselage one could avoid the hostility and isolation of the desert simply by leaping over it. The first municipal airport opened in 1925 six miles outside of the city, but it was never a commercial success. However, several private airfields also developed, which were more successful, and in 1927 the first scheduled flights began to operate from one of these.[1] In November of 1928, a company called Scenic Airways bought an airfield two miles east of downtown between 24th and 32nd Streets and named it Sky Harbor. The name invoked the future of air travel: airplanes would perform the historic function that a desert city had always lacked. Other commercial carriers joined in using this facility, and the city acquired the airport in 1935.[2]

Clear skies, a dry climate, level ground, reasonable elevation, and the lack of high wind made Phoenix exceptionally well suited to flying. As early as 1939 the area became a center for pilot training. In January 1941, *The Arizona Republic* announced a federal plan to establish a major advanced training facility near Glendale. Del Webb built the facility, which ultimately became Luke Field.[3] By the end of the war Luke was the world's largest advanced flight school, having trained nearly 14,000 pilots. Del Webb was also selected to build Higley Field, a military airport that was later renamed Williams Field.

Concurrently, Los Angeles was becoming a worldwide hub for the aircraft manufacturing industry. Phoenix's proximity to the Los Angeles metropolitan area meant that it received some defense contracting business. Paul Litchfield of the Goodyear Tire and Rubber Company helped to develop a government-owned electronics plant in the West Valley. Litchfield noted one of the justifications for the Arizona location: "It is well inland and thus protected from any possible air attacks."[4] The arrival of this plant was seen by the Chamber of Commerce and other Phoenix boosters as pivotal in turning Phoenix into an industrial center.

The war became an enormous magnet that attracted Americans to California and Texas to work in defense-related industries. During the 1940s essentially every new Westerner was an urban dweller drawn by growth in war industries.[5] While aircraft building and defense contracting did not have the immediate impact on Phoenix that it did on California and Texas, the reality of air travel after the war began to transform the city. Shipping by air could be cost efficient for small high-value goods. As the huge defense industries began looking for civilian business opportunities, electronics manufacturing companies realized that with air travel, manufacturing plants could locate away from conventional transportation routes. The commercial airlines, which resulted from the expertise in manufacturing and flying developed during the war, were looking for goods and people to transport. Passenger travel by air exploded after the war, from fewer than 600,000 passengers in 1934 to nearly 15,000,000 in 1948.[6]

Airline travel is a force of concentration on urban form. A train can make multiple stops with relative efficiency and incremental additional expense. But in air travel, multiple stops are to be avoided because of the penalty in cost and delay. Speed is the benefit of travel by air, and that benefit is greatest with fewer stops. The pricing mechanisms used by air transportation makes this clear—short trips are proportionately far more expensive. So air travel had the effect of concentrating business activity in fewer, larger cities with substantial airports. Those cities became dominant centers of regional areas, with the big airport being the hub of other transportation modes. Jet travel further increased the concentrating effect.

In 1948, recognizing the growing accessibility of a city well served by air, Motorola decided to open a Phoenix facility specializing in defense electronics. The impact of that decision on the Valley of the Sun is almost impossible to overstate. Not only did it form the first outpost of electronics manufacturing in what would come to be known as the "silicon desert," but it also had an immediate effect on the second technological advance that made modern Phoenix possible: air conditioning.

Since the earliest days of settlement, Phoenicians had sought a way to insulate themselves from the summer's heat. Ironically, continuing to use the indigenous construction of thick-walled small-windowed adobe buildings rejected by the early settlers as uncivilized would have provided some help. Sleeping porches were a partial response to the climate, since the dry desert cooled down at night. On those porches, citizens might find the only way to go to sleep was to wrap themselves in wet sheets before laying down on a bed or cot or to hang those wet sheets up around the edge of the porch, creating a primitive form of evaporative cooling.

Combining the wet sheet with an electric fan created the earliest successful mechanical device for home cooling. The evaporative coolers created by such pioneers as the Goettl and Palmer families became a thriving local industry, which shipped evaporative coolers around the drier parts of the

John F. Long took every opportunity to promote his air-conditioned homes.
John F. Long

nation.[7] An evaporative cooler cooled the air by injecting water into it, raising the humidity. As a result, it did not work when the humidity went above about 15 or 20 percent. This meant it was not useful for cooling most of the southern United States and it also was not as effective in Phoenix when the late summer monsoon caused the humidity to rise.

What is today recognized as an air conditioner—a machine that cools the air while dehumidifying—had been essentially invented in 1902 by Willis Carrier.[8] He built the machine for a printing company in Brooklyn, New York, in order to reduce the humidity in the plant, which was distorting color in the printing process. Most of the early applications of air conditioning were for major industrial buildings, since the machines were huge, expensive, and dangerous because the coolant was a toxic ammonia compound. As refrigerant chemicals were improved and as the units became more manageable in size, air conditioners moved into office buildings. Air conditioning began to penetrate the American consciousness when it started arriving in movie theaters in the early 1920s. The ritual of the summertime movie as a way to escape oppressive heat remains etched on our collective memory to this day.

The first widespread application of air conditioning to houses were window units, which first appeared after World War II. Sales jumped from 75,000 in 1948 to more than a million by 1953. "The dripping box jutting out of the bedroom window joined the TV aerial on the roof as instant fixtures in the American suburban landscape."[9] In Phoenix, the window unit appeared first in the master bedroom so that mom and dad could get to sleep at night. Children growing up in post-war Phoenix would be allowed to play in the master bedroom in the daytime because it was the only part of the house that was comfortable. At night, the kids still had to settle for the evaporative cooler. By the end of the 1940s, Phoenix led the nation in the number of home air conditioning units installed. Promoters who in the past had gone out of their way to avoid mentioning hot summers now explained that air conditioning made Phoenix like anywhere else in the country.

Central home air conditioning gained acceptance more slowly, in part due to cost. Initially, the FHA was unwilling to accept central air as part of its mortgages. When the agency reversed itself in 1957, installation boomed.[10] The 1960 census reported that in Phoenix more households had central air than window units—nearly 25 percent of all houses. Carrier corporate statistics indicated that nearly half of all spec houses nationally had central air by 1960.[11]

Motorola became Phoenix's biggest booster, and the company could personally attest to air conditioning's transformation of the city's desert conditions. In establishing its manufacturing plants, Motorola found the low humidity climate to be an advantage. Motorola's plants had to be air conditioned in order to provide the dust-free environment necessary for manufacturing. They also liked the fact that, unlike at their headquarters near Chicago, there were rarely weather problems that prevented their employees from getting to work. Absenteeism fell and they had little problem attracting employees to Phoenix.[12] Those employees began working in the air-conditioned plants Motorola had built and they saw no reason why their houses should not be fully air conditioned as well. Dan Noble, executive vice president of Motorola and the principal motivator in the company coming to Phoenix, wrote in 1954:

> Experience with evaporative coolers showed that they worked very well the greater part of the time, but that refrigeration in the laboratories insures perpetually satisfactory working conditions for the staff during the summer months. . . . Staff members are installing refrigeration units in their homes to provide an equally satisfactory control of temperatures for the family. . . . Motorola management feels that refrigeration cooling is the complete solution to the Phoenix summer heat problem. Refrigeration cooling has transformed Phoenix into a year-round city of delightful living.[13]

Ironically, Phoenix's most famous part-time resident of the 1950s, Frank Lloyd Wright, hated the technology that made Phoenix habitable. It made designing in the desert less of a challenge, and removed a measure of the "organic" basis of good architecture. However valid his point, it did not stop the population from falling in love with air conditioning. Refrigeration brought an extended tourist season and made the city more comfortable for residents to stay in town during the summer. Many of the military veterans who had served in the area came back to live in air-conditioned comfort. By the 1950s air conditioners even began showing up in automobiles.

Air conditioning had enormous social impacts on the development of post-war America. The rise of the Sunbelt as the center for American growth in the 1960s coincides with market penetration by central air conditioning. Air conditioning enabled people living in Houston or Atlanta or Phoenix to dress like people in New York or Chicago and to shop for the same kinds of soft goods. The physical appearance of communities also changed to adapt to the new technology. The demise of neighborhood sociability represented in the loss of the front porch is often blamed on the automobile. But in fact air conditioning and television had far more impact on where Americans chose to spend their time when at home. No longer was it necessary to sit out in the evening to cool off. Inside, there was comfort and entertainment.

Air conditioning finally allowed Phoenix to become the American metropolis it had aspired to be. During the 1950s the city's population increased by 311 percent, the highest rate of growth among the nation's 50 largest cities. In 1959 there was more construction in Phoenix than in the years from 1914 to 1946. A total of more than 5,000 single-family residences were built. By 1960 it was the largest city in the Southwest, with a population of 439,000.

Annexation was a vital part of Phoenix's population growth. By the mid-twentieth century, the plight of many Eastern urban areas was becoming clear: growth on the edge was attracting the new suburban homeowner. A middle class wage earner who would have been a lifetime renter before the war was able, with government-backed financing, to purchase a home for the first time. New suburban homes were being built rapidly and relatively efficiently, thanks largely to the success of the government policies that had focused on revolutionizing a "backward" industry. In addition, the auto industry had built huge manufacturing capacity during the war, and was able to produce large numbers of cars in a variety of styles, sizes, and price ranges well suited to the rising middle class.

In well-established urban areas, this emerging pattern of homeownership meant that many rural communities were being transformed into bedroom

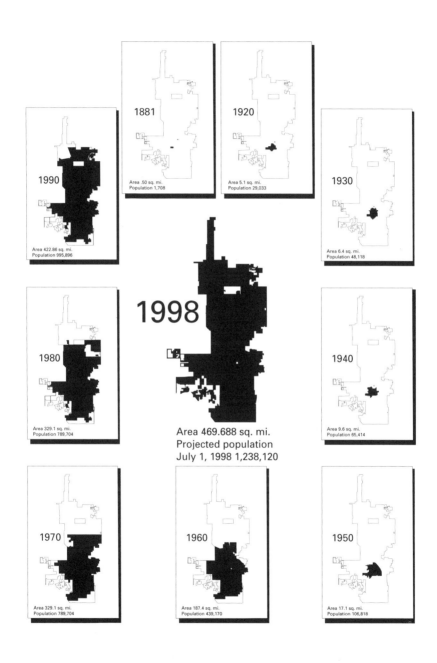

City of Phoenix growth, 1881–1998.
City of Phoenix Planning Department

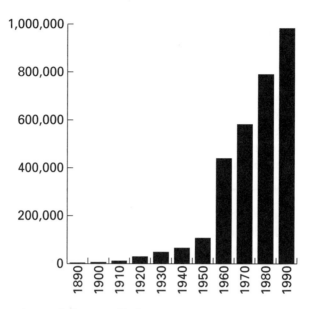

City of Phoenix population growth.
City of Phoenix

suburbs. The established big city was often landlocked by smaller existing municipalities or by natural boundaries such as rivers, lakes, or coasts. Suburban growth became a drain on the central city, which began a gradual demographic decline. With that decline came an erosion of revenues. Urban redevelopment got its start as the established cities tried to reverse the increasingly apparent trend.

Phoenix faced a different reality. It did not have the traditional historic core of a major city. In 1950, it ranked only as the ninety-ninth largest city in America, with a population of just over 100,000. The city's pre-war downtown, such as it was, was that of a small midwestern city. Nor did Phoenix have either geographic or political boundaries to keep it from expanding. Watching what was happening around the country, the city's leadership realized that they had a choice. They could allow the city to be surrounded by satellites that might grow at its expense, or embark an aggressive annexation to expand the City of Phoenix's boundaries as the Valley grew. The existing cities of Tempe, Scottsdale, Mesa, and Glendale did create some limits, but those communities were themselves able to expand through annexation. In other directions, especially to the north, Phoenix had a clear path to extend its geographic borders. Beginning in 1956, the elected officials of Phoenix set out on a conscious course to avoid being hemmed in by a group of independent suburbs.[14] In 1940 Phoenix had covered an area of

9.6 square miles. By 1955 it covered 29 square miles, and by 1960, 187 square miles. The annexation program was so aggressive that by 1960, 75 percent of the people living in the city limits were residents of areas that had been annexed in the previous ten years.

As the city was vigorously annexing, it was finally able to attract the large numbers of new businesses and residents that the community's real estate sector had so long sought. Promotion remained an extremely high priority for the city's leaders. El Paso, the Sunbelt city that Phoenix had eclipsed, even admitted that business leadership in Phoenix had been way in front in doing a "selling job of the Phoenix metropolitan area."[15]

The war years had been a time of austerity for America. Architecture responded to the government's war needs and tended toward the utilitarian. Domestic production of automobiles had been halted or frozen, with no energy going into new designs. Once the war ended, euphoria over America's future role filled the country with a kind of space-age optimism. New technologies and production capabilities in all industries were available, and so the era spawned exuberant roadside architecture to match the tailfins being installed on the backs of cars. Coffee shops with boomerang signs caught the attention of motorists moving by at 50 miles per hour.[16] While the wilder expressions of a roadside pop architecture were relatively short lived, the great trends of post-war city development were unabashedly automobile oriented.

The two most pervasive post-war developments in architecture were the shopping center and the ranch house. Together these building forms changed the nature of how American cities grew and looked. They became the building blocks of metropolitan Phoenix and most of the cities of the modern West. Exactly what constitutes a shopping center, as opposed to a collection of individual shops, is open to interpretation. Today, the commonly accepted definition requires a group of architecturally unified buildings built on a site that is planned, developed, and managed as a single entity.[17] Historically, the distinguishing characteristic of a shopping center was highly visible accessible parking shared by several different stores. When shopping became a motorized rather than a pedestrian activity, storefronts were ultimately pushed away from the street because the visibility of parking became more of an attraction than the visibility of merchandise. The physical appearance of communities was transformed by that single design change.

In Phoenix, an infatuation with visible surface parking came in the late 1920s, a remarkably early date. When the A. J. Bayless market chain opened its seventh store in March 1928, it set the building back 35 feet from the curb line in order to provide ample parking room for "several score" automobiles

An early corner shopping center surrounded by single-family homes.
John F. Long

in a "provision which thus has been made for motoring shoppers [which] will prevent congestion of parked machines in [the] streets near the store. . . ."[18]

Bayless's new market was 8,000 square feet, the largest it had ever built, and an example of the growing phenomenon of the supermarket. From an early Piggly Wiggly self-service store in Memphis in 1916, the supermarket spread across America.[19] After World War I, the average household was able to acquire a refrigerator, an appliance which revolutionized shopping habits. A housewife equipped with a refrigerator, and later a freezer, was freed from having to shop every day. A weekly shopping trip meant there were too many bags to be carried at once, and a car was necessary to transport the groceries. The needed parking meant that large supermarkets were not suited to downtown locations. Also, since you had to push a shopping cart around to collect a week's worth of groceries, the store had to be located all on one floor—an inefficient use of expensive downtown land.

The supermarket became the anchor of the shopping center, which added an assortment of other often-frequented shopping destinations, all of which could be visited on a single trip. In 1907 a multi-tenant retail commercial building set back from the street was built in Baltimore, and may have been the country's earliest shopping center.[20] The earliest documented center in Phoenix was the Publix Market, built at 7th Street and Roosevelt Street in 1929. An L-shaped building of Mission Revival style, it was the first drive-in market in Phoenix.[21]

As suburban housing began to boom, the shopping center became an integral part of growth. In 1950, there were only 100 neighborhood shopping centers in the United States. By 1953, the number had tripled, and by 1960 there were 3,700.[22] Uptown Plaza at Central Avenue and Camelback Road was probably the first complex in Phoenix to capture the full force of this retailing phenomenon. When it opened in 1955, it occupied a ten-acre site, and was billed as the largest single shopping center between Dallas and Los Angeles.[23]

As Phoenix began its rapid annexation program, the national trend toward business and retail decentralization was in full swing. Street cars in Phoenix stopped operating in 1948 and it was the automobile that provided the means to expand the city's physical boundaries. The flat topography and one-mile grid of farm roads created a simple formula for urbanization. The intersections of two section-line arterial roads provided perfect locations for dispersed retail shopping centers, gas stations, and convenience restaurants. A development pattern began to emerge—a developer would acquire a quarter section or more of land and subdivide it for houses, holding out a ten-acre parcel on the corner for a shopping center. A commercial developer, often with a supermarket anchor tenant already committed, would build the center several years later. By 1957, aerial photos of the City of Phoenix make this pattern clear: at least two dozen section-line corner shopping centers are in operation, with at least as many vacant sites surrounded by subdivisions.[24]

It is tempting but inaccurate to think of the growth that occurred in Phoenix and the Southwest in the 1950s and 1960s as being unprecedented in American history. In fact, between 1850 and 1890, Chicago grew from 29,000 people to more than one million. The difference was that the postwar growth of Phoenix and the urban Southwest was accommodated in the low-density urban fabric of dispersed employment and retail and, above all, detached single-family homes.

The concerns about home ownership had to be put on hold during the war, as the building industry was virtually ignored. Housing starts during the war years fell from one million nationally to fewer than 100,000.[25] Rising birth rates and returning GIs put enormous demands on housing after the war, and the speed and efficiency which had been applied to war production provided new lessons for homebuilding. The federal government's earlier efforts to revive homebuilding had enormous impact on construction in the post-war era. Easy financing programs under the FHA and the VA in combination with the attention paid to new home construction by popular magazines, architects, and manufacturers spurred the largest increase in homebuilding in American history. The FHA and the VA adopted design and construction standards in order to keep costs within reason and standardize building practices. Such standardization included prefabricated window units, composition board, and improved drywall.

FHA and VA mortgages were also designed to keep houses within reach of as many Americans as possible. Immediately after the war, returning GIs and the families they established expected to be able to buy houses. They even had an expectation about cost: about two years' wages—around $5,000 to $6,000.[26] The first director of the FHA for southern California and Arizona, Fred Marlow, a real estate developer from Los Angeles, had been a vocal critic of any government involvement in housing. Once he took the federal job, he became a zealous advocate for the "volume market," challenging builders to produce houses selling for less than $3,500:

> Right there is the biggest market . . . just as the auto industry met the same mass marketing, deluged it with fine low priced cars and put the whole nation on wheels, so the housing industry must build good houses for the masses at prices they can afford. The real estate fraternity can sell this market by offering an acceptable product at the right price. This does not mean the building industry must content itself with lower profits. Rather, it may find it better business to narrow the profit margin on unit sales and build more units.[27]

The houses, which would become the units of production, needed to be simple, efficient, easy to build in volume, and suited to the automobile-oriented suburbs. The evolution into integrated land development and homebuilding had proved successful, and it was in this developer-driven model that the homes needed to meet post-war demand could be built. Developers wanted models that required little architectural input after the initial design. To the problem of providing houses in large numbers, a new science was applied—market research. Between 1936 and 1950, dozens of large-scale consumer housing surveys were run by the mass-market family and ladies' magazines.[28] These surveys looked at citizens as consumers and houses as products that needed to be tailored to meet the market. They revealed that people wanted lots with a place for the kids to play, kitchens that opened to the rest of the home, and an informal "family" room where children could feel comfortable and the television could be the focus of family life. Bedrooms should be a separate private zone and more than one bathroom was expected.[29] When these preferences for a more open floor plan and private yard merged with the need for efficient low-cost production, a suitable style emerged—the ranch house.

A typical modest Phoenix ranch house from the early 1950s.

The ranch house was in part a repudiation of the make-believe world of period revival housing. The harsh reality of World War II had brought everyone back to understanding the need for simple inexpensive housing in contrast to "fancied up" French or Colonial styles. Ranch-style architecture was rooted deeply in the Western soil and well adapted to the Western climate. Patios and wide porches were common in the early indigenous architectural forms of the West, especially in California. It is probable that the earliest adaptations of ranch house form to modern housing were in the early 1930s in both southern and northern California.[30] The early prototypes have been related to the California bungalow style as well as to the vernacular Spanish rural house. The houses were one story, with a low pitched roof, generous overhangs, and simple construction materials. Outdoor living areas were integrated into the structure, "underscoring the important principle of providing an easy relationship with the out-of-doors."[31]

In the post-war boom, California architect Cliff May and *Sunset* had the broadest influence in making the ranch house the new model for the ubiquitous suburban residence. May and *Sunset* published a series of simple plans featuring a living room, separate family room, patio for outdoor entertaining, and attached carport that was entered from the front of the house. *Sunset* even identified one characteristic of the style as presenting a relatively blank facade to the street, in historical reference to the arid climate preference for private living space in patios and backyards.[32] May was a celebrated custom home architect of the period, but he was also at the forefront of the mass marketing of the ranch house, producing a 1953 prefabricated version of an 815-square-foot house that sold for $7,500.[33]

Ranch houses arrived early in Phoenix. In 1936 an advertisement in *The Arizona Republic* featured such a house, calling it a "southwestern bungalow," though today it would be recognized as a quintessential ranch home.[34] Early ranch houses in Phoenix incorporated elements of the California ranch, or in some cases had Spanish Colonial or even French Provincial overtones.[35] The eventual mass-produced ranch house was a simpler structure, one story with a box or L-shape, usually built of painted or unpainted brick with metal casement windows, a shallow front porch, and overhanging eaves with exposed rafter ends. As Jeffrey Cook and others have pointed out, the typical mass-produced Phoenix ranch house, which combined these elements with an attached carport, slab-on-grade construction, and an open floor plan, was in fact a relatively mature and intelligent building form for the desert environment.[36]

At the same time the individual ranch house design was being refined for mass marketing, the policies of the FHA were also influencing the larger context of neighborhood planning. The FHA's standards moved beyond individual buildings into their relationship to one another, with the notion that a streetscape should present an appearance of uniformity and design continuity so as to uphold property values.[37] This planning concept was a continuation of the efforts of the FHA to standardize building practices and to reduce costs. It was also indicative of the shift that occurred in the role of the developer from land subdivider to community builder. In order to maintain FHA support for a development, many Phoenix builders began to construct standardized homes that adhered to the construction and livability requirements of the FHA and that incorporated covenants to ensure neighborhood consistency and uniformity. The achievements of Bill Levitt in mass-producing community have been well documented.[38] At Levittown, New York, he built 17,000 homes after the war, delivering the suburban lifestyle starting at $7,990. Phoenix in the 1950s had an analogue: John F. Long.[39]

In 1947, as a returning veteran, Long built a single house for himself and his wife Mary. Before they could move in, they were offered a price which represented a profit of nearly 50 percent, and sold it for $8,000. Within two years Long had become a tract home builder, starting with a 90-lot subdivision. By 1952, a Phoenix FHA official called Long's houses "the best value in town" and another FHA man in Washington said "no one in the country can touch him." The following year, he built 305 houses, and by 1956 his annual volume was 1,000 at a time when the average builder constructed between five and ten homes.[40] Long's "Mayfair" model used board and batten over concrete block to emphasize the "ranch" look, and for $9,800 the buyer got 1,220 square feet of living area, three bedrooms, living and family rooms, and a carport or garage.

This Attractive
SOUTHWESTERN BUNGALOW
With Two-Car Garage

Can Be Built for Only . . . **$65.11★** A Month

This monthly payment includes principal, interest, service charge, insurance and taxes, (state, county and city and school district), based on the Kenilworth district. It will therefore vary a few dollars a month according to the tax rate of the locality in which it is built.

Build With a F. H. A. Loan

Cost of home illustrated $6,500
Assume prospective builder owns lot valued at . . $ 650

Total value of house and lot $7,150
80% F.H.A. Loan on total valuation $5,700

THE beautiful home illustrated, showing its attractive exterior and convenient floor plan, is ideally adapted to this locality. It is roomy, homey, and will be especially appealing to those who want the utmost in comfort that modern innovations bring.

Constructed with wood studs, with plaster exterior, it can be finished in many different colors that adapt themselves to the residential section in which it is built. The type of construction also provides the means to incorporate the best of insulation. The roof, of wood shingles, and the picturesque shutters may be finished to contrast with the other exterior finishes. The brick front porch, which the plan suggests, adds another modern touch.

This house may give you ideas which you can incorporate in the home you have planned to build. So study the drawing carefully. Note the number of rooms, how the home is built to give utmost in ventilation, and to provide outside space which is so desirable in a home-place!

If your home plans are now crystalized, learn of the easy financing plans available. You can start your own home before a new year rolls around, if you act at once.

★ Complete air conditioning . . . cooling in summer and gas heating in winter . . . may be installed in one compact unit for a very few dollars per month . . . for FREE advice or consulting service to homebuilders and architects, call the Air Conditioning Department of the Power Company. Phone 3-3121.

TAKE 19½ YEARS TO PAY..!

FHA SINGLE MORTGAGE SYSTEM

How to Finance Your Home

You can qualify for a loan if you have a regular income and can show at least 20 per cent equity in the value of a house and lot combined by cash, trade or ownership of a lot . . . See a lumber dealer or tradesman . . . $16,000 is the highest amount loaned which can not exceed 80 per cent of the appraised value of the property . . . Loan may run any number of years, but not to exceed 20 years . . . Interest charged on loans for new construction is 5 per cent . . . Monthly payments include all charges and payments on principal.

A 1930s advertisement for a Phoenix-area home.
The Arizona Republic November 8, 1936

John F. Long's impact was not just in the design or construction of individual houses. In 1953, he assembled 2,000 acres in 20 tracts for a planned community he named Maryvale after his wife. He hired Los Angeles architect and planner Victor Gruen to lay out a master plan, which included schools, parks, employment areas, and shopping centers. The community opened in 1955 with a carnival-like event called "The Greatest Home Show on Earth." In the first week 24,000 people visited the models. Billboards heralded three-bedroom two-bath homes for $7,950 and homes with swimming pools for $9,800. The event was covered in *Life*, *Time*, *McCall's*, *Better Homes and Gardens*, and *House and Home*. Eventually Maryvale grew to house 100,000 people, which at the time would have made it the third-largest city in Arizona had it not been part of the City of Phoenix.

In 1958, John F. Long was recognized as the number one low-cost homebuilder in America. *American Builder* magazine featured a 15-page spread explaining how Long's mass production methods enabled him to deliver more house for the money than anyone in the country.[41] Houses were designed from the inside out to maximize room sizes but use the minimum amount of building materials. A fully integrated organization avoided the use of subcontractors whenever possible. Long was among the first builders in the country to use prefab plumbing trees, prefab roof trusses, and even prefab wall sections. The company built all its own cabinets and countertops. Long's shops developed the first machine to continuously pour sidewalk and rolled curb.

Long was also an innovator in financing his homes. He pioneered the use of an FHA housing program known as Section 213. Under this program, Long's subdivisions were built in cooperative units of 40 to 50 houses. Buyers held shares in the co-op, and a majority of the houses had to be presold. At the end of construction, all the houses were simultaneously transferred to the buyers with separate 40-year mortgages. This technique minimized interim financing costs and allowed lower down payments. In many cases, the houses appraised so much higher than the sales price that no down payment was required. In 1959, Long testified in Congress in support of a proposal that would allow parks and other community facilities to be added into the co-op financing. The Senate committee was so impressed with the value of his houses, they reprinted the plans in the *Congressional Record*.[42]

By the end of the 1950s, John F. Long's organization was selling more than 2,500 homes a year. He was moving increasingly toward factory-like production with constructed components assembled in the field. His goal, he said, "was that the guys in the field would never look at a blueprint— that just slows things down."[43] Between 1947 and 1975 he built 30,000 houses priced at no more than $30,000 each.

Residents lined up to see the houses featured in John F. Long's Maryvale.
John F. Long

Long's Maryvale is a preeminent example of the suburban developments that symbolize American life in the 1950s and 1960s. While numerous social critics "gleefully lambasted ranch house developments as the tasteless hallmark of a homogenized society," most of the new suburban dwellers were reasonably content with the homes they bought.[44] The ranch house suburbs brought home ownership to a broader range of Americans than ever before—and made it a defining characteristic of middle class status. Mass production techniques kept it affordable and created the new phenomenon of the starter home. The young families of the 1950s looked forward to increased buying power as they matured. As that happened, they assumed they would move on to newer and larger houses rather than staying in place as previous generations had done. Houses were simply one more part of their lives as increasingly affluent consumers.[45]

Phoenix was a stunning success in this new consumer world. In 1954 the mortgage banking association held a meeting in Phoenix, and one participant gushed: "I have no hesitancy in stating now that, in my opinion, more house per dollar is delivered in the Phoenix area than in any other section of the country that I have visited." "[S]o far I have not seen anything anywhere to compare with what your local builders produce and sell both from a financial standpoint and architecturally speaking. . . . I well remember when I first visited Phoenix and inspected the houses being built by Long, Hall, and Riskas and at first sight found it very difficult to believe what I saw," said another.[46]

The Phoenix formula had finally been found. Air travel, air conditioning, shopping centers, and, especially, affordable mass-produced houses made Phoenix the fastest growing city in the country. In the two years just before 1960, 44,000 building permits were issued in Maricopa County for single-family dwellings. By 1960, the city's population of 440,000 propelled it into the top 50 U.S. cities for the first time. During the 1960s and 1970s, the concept of the master-planned ranch house subdivision with Bermuda grass lawns was replicated again and again, as the population of the City of Phoenix climbed to 581,000 in 1970 and 790,000 in 1980. Phoenix embodied the post-war dream.

Careful What You Wish For ─────────

The recent past is invariably the most treacherous because, lacking perspective, we understand it the least. Active participants have their view further distorted by the rationalization of personal behavior. But in trying to understand metropolitan Phoenix, the story cannot be stopped in the late 1970s—too much has happened since. Between 1980 and 1990, the metropolitan area grew by 40 percent, to 2.2 million, and the City of Phoenix itself reached 983,000. By 1997, the city was estimated to have 1,159,014 residents, making it sixth in population in the nation; the metropolitan area was fifteenth, with 2,839,539.[1]

Besides sunshine and reasonably priced houses, extraordinary job creation drove this growth. In 1950, 17,000 area residents were employed in manufacturing. Ten years later, the number reached nearly 50,000. By 1997, 208,000 were employed in manufacturing. Service industries, tourism, and government similarly exploded, while the traditional industries of mining and agriculture were flat or in decline. In the mid-1990s, 60,000 to 70,000 jobs were being created in the metropolitan area each year, usually ranking in the top five nationally.

Throughout this period of growth, the City of Phoenix continued its aggressive annexation policies to absorb new developments and, in 1997, the city's 469 square miles passed Los Angeles to make it eighth in size in the nation. Residents of metropolitan Phoenix became accustomed to hearing that the area was either number one or two nationally in single-family housing permits, and often near the top in retail and industrial permitting as well. At various times, Scottsdale, Chandler, Mesa, or Gilbert might be the single fastest growing city in America.

Even as in-migration fed the state's growth, large numbers of the newcomers did not stay. During the 1980s, three left for every five who arrived.[2] Out-migration rates were higher than for economically depressed rust belt areas.[3] Rapid growth led to a desert encampment-style city—residents thinking of themselves as from "back home" and on the way to somewhere else. The high turnover in population led to political instability. Voters without a long political memory made it easy for a variety of untested and even unknown politicians to rise to power. Sometimes the result brought unfavorable national publicity to the state: Evan Mecham, AzScam, the Super Bowl and Martin Luther King Day, Fife Symington.

By the 1990s, metropolitan Phoenix was caught in the crisis of getting what it wanted. Growth became the activity most basic to the city's self-image and simultaneously the activity most threatening to the city's survival: the raison d'être and the curse. Deep ambivalence about growth and community character became increasingly evident. Was this place really a city or only a suburb in search of an urb? Did the area need freeways, buses, or monorails? Was density good or bad? What about tall buildings? Should Phoenix look more like other American cities? What about sprawl? Was downtown important? Behavior, attitudes, and decisions reflecting the conflicting attitudes toward continued growth were especially evident in debates about transportation and urban form.

Phoenix is often described as the "epitome of post–World War II western auto-oriented suburban development."[4] Yet, uncharacteristically for such a place, Phoenix grew into a big city without a meaningful freeway system. Starting in the 1950s, civic leaders began studying the experience with freeways in California and planning for the interstate highway link into Phoenix. A 1960 plan had recommended development of 140 miles of freeways, but by 1977 only 40 miles had been built. In 1967, most cities the size of metro Phoenix carried five times more traffic on freeways.

The reason for Phoenix's reluctance to embrace freeways was a complex mixture of politics, timing, and fortuitous geography. Historically, the city placed great reliance on the federal government for support of growth, yet it showed a remarkable willingness to pass up much of the federal freeway money that was available. In contrast to the area's attitude about water projects, the opportunity to access outside money took second place to fighting about exactly where the freeways should be and what they should look like.

The consequences of the lack of freeways were not felt for many years. Throughout the 1960s and 1970s, as the metropolitan area expanded, it continued to be well served by the forgiving nature of its one-mile supergrid of streets. Those streets provided the average Phoenician with a variety of routes to work and elsewhere. The grid was easy to build as needed: farm roads were expanded as subdivisions replaced cotton fields. Little advance planning was necessary, and there was no requirement for a massive investment in street infrastructure. As the roads were expanded, sewer, water, and utilities would also be extended, often at the cost of the developer.

In 1960, a consultant from San Francisco, Wilbur Smith and Associates, produced a plan calling for 140 miles of freeway to be built. But the price tag of nearly $550 million was too high, and the business community did not embrace the plan. Only the Black Canyon/Maricopa Interstate was constructed during the 1960s, giving the metropolitan area a single linear controlled-access highway.

Eventually, the impact of more people and cars began to take its toll. Traffic congestion continued to increase on the arterial streets, despite constant widening. By 1966, the average peak-hour speed had dropped to 26 miles per hour from just over 30 miles per hour in 1958. In 1968, a report

Model of the original proposed Papago Inner Loop, including one of the helicoils.
Phoenix Newspapers, Inc.

from the Arizona Department of Transportation and the Maricopa Association of Governments proposed a supergrid of freeways for the greater Phoenix area. The plan, prepared by a team of consultants, extolled the virtues of freeways in other cities and recited the negative comparisons to Phoenix's situation. The failure to act, it suggested, would mean that Phoenix would fall behind in quality of life. The plan also proposed a radical design feature: through the heart of the city, crossing Central Avenue between downtown and the uptown area near Park Central Mall, the road (known as the Papago Inner Loop) would be elevated on stilts 100 feet in the air. It would give Phoenix a visual landmark, they suggested, equivalent to the Golden Gate Bridge or the St. Louis Gateway Arch. The elevated solution was cheaper than going below grade, and by being so high it was hoped that there would be no "visual barrier" dividing the city. But getting off the freeway would require driving on spring-like "helicoils."[5]

Opposition to the plan immediately surfaced. By the late 1960s, urban freeways were a mature enough phenomenon that their negative effects in dividing parts of the city and in seeming to increase, not decrease, traffic congestion were well known. A group called Citizens for Mass Transit Against Freeways was formed to protest what they saw as likely increases in air pollution and blight. They received support from an unlikely quarter: *The Arizona Republic*.

Initially, the *Republic* had offered tepid support for the freeway, criticizing only its extension into Papago Park. But in late 1972 Eugene Pulliam, the publisher of both the *Republic* and the *Gazette* and arguably the single most influential person in Arizona at that time, decided to launch a crusade against the inner loop.

The reasons for Pulliam's attitude were complex. He disliked the elevated design, he distrusted land speculators who were buying in the right-of-way, he believed freeways had been a negative influence on Los Angeles. But most important, he and his wife, Nina, thought freeways would change the quality of life in Phoenix: "I don't care if we grow in our density pattern all the way to Wickenburg," former Mayor Driggs quoted Pulliam as saying. "That would be better than the environmental change to our lifestyle that would occur from a major urban freeway program."[6]

Never before had the establishment in Phoenix been so visibly split on an issue related to growth. The city council and most of the business community supported the freeways but, led by Pulliam, the newspapers were relentless—not only editorializing against the proposal, but running photos of Los Angeles smog and congestion on page one day after day.[7] Feeling the pressure, the city council finally agreed to put the issue on a public ballot for an advisory vote in 1973, hoping to get a favorable endorsement before public sentiment eroded further. In the end, Pulliam won—the Papago was rejected by 58 percent of the voters.

An initiative petition drive launched in 1975 brought the issue of freeways back on the ballot, this time with the inner loop at ground level. The newspapers still opposed the measure, but Pulliam died before the campaign started and, without the freeway on stilts, the voters thought it would be acceptable. A third public vote in 1979 again endorsed the Papago (which, by then, was supported even by the *Republic*), and it ultimately received federal funding by becoming part of the Interstate Highway System. With federal dollars, it could be built underground with a park on top. The inner loop was the last piece of the cross-country highway system to be built.

Not until 1985 did growing traffic congestion convince Maricopa County voters to pass a proposition dedicating a half percent sales tax for a larger network of freeway construction (with a smaller percentage dedicated to mass transit). A broad coalition of business and community leaders mounted a massive campaign on behalf of the ballot proposition. At the time the sales tax for freeways passed, Phoenix had only 70 miles of freeway, making the metropolitan area dead last in number of freeway miles among the 75 largest metropolitan areas in the country. The sales tax increase was to fund 233 miles of freeway, and the Maricopa Association of Governments (MAG) developed a plan calling for a regional network of 320 miles by the year 2005.

The freeways built between 1986 and 1995 as a result of this infusion of local money had dramatic short-term impacts on traffic congestion. Between 1988 and 1992, Phoenix increased both freeway and major street capacity more than any other urbanized area in the United States and was one of two urban areas to actually reduce traffic congestion. During that time period, Phoenix dropped from being the fourth most congested major city to being twenty-first.[8]

Financial problems ultimately beset the freeway plan and costs, especially for land acquisition, increased while tax revenues decreased in the recession of the late 1980s. In March 1989 the region's voters were asked to increase the sales tax dedicated to transportation to 1 percent. Part of the money would be used for an ambitious and complex 103-mile rail system called ValTrans. City councils throughout the Valley feared that being left out of the new system would doom the future of their city. In order to buy their support, MAG expanded and expanded its vision of the system. Ultimately, it grew so large as to undermine the already thin support in the electorate, and the plan was defeated by a three-to-two margin. The voters' message seemed to be explicitly anti-transit. The plan was simply too grandiose; it did not appear realistic in a city with such low existing transit ridership, and most voters could not imagine actually using the system.

In 1994, freeway construction was again on the ballot, with transit as a much less visible part of the package. This time the voters were not very interested in transit, but again soundly defeated the measure because of a perception that the existing program had been mismanaged. Subsequently, the upturn in the economy raised sales tax revenues, providing more money for freeway construction. After readjusting priorities, the revised system is projected to be completed in 2014. As to transit, after the failures of two regional approaches, several Valley cities decided to go their own way. Tempe was successful, but both Scottsdale and Phoenix measures lost in September 1997, in Phoenix's case by fewer than 200 votes. Meanwhile, civic and business leaders began to regroup to figure out how to address once again the issue of public transportation, believing that Phoenix's last place in transit miles and financial support for transit among America's big cities was unacceptable.

The private automobile has been an inextricable part of facilitating the boom of metropolitan Phoenix. As the city grew, incremental investment in surface streets was a simple, cost-effective solution to facilitating and reinforcing the dominant growth pattern of single-family homes. The recent history of voter reaction to transportation issues suggests that the message continues to be: We like our lifestyle of low-density personal mobility and want to change only by the minimum increment necessary to avoid serious deterioration to that lifestyle. Don't talk to us about grand visions of transforming how we get around, just keep traffic moving.

The same citizenry that is skeptical about changing its transportation habits has been equally ambivalent in its attitudes toward concentrations of intense activity, tall buildings, and other traditional particulars of urban life. Whether areas of intense development are desirable in a metropolitan area of low-density urban form has been repeatedly debated. In the City of Phoenix, this debate has centered on areas called village cores.

Downtown Phoenix had been a respectable retail core until the 1950s, but it never developed the uses and amenities beyond what would be found in any small city. Then, as Phoenix began its dramatic growth curve, downtown was left behind by the evolution of shopping centers into regional malls. The first department store–anchored center in Phoenix, Park Central Mall, was built in 1957 three miles north of downtown. It opened with Goldwater's and Diamond's, the city's two principal department stores. Chris-Town Mall (1961) and Scottsdale Fashion Square (1962) moved major retail further into the suburbs. By the late 1960s, there were no department stores left in downtown.[9]

This paralleled a national trend in which new stores were built only as mall anchors. Regional mall locations were dictated by major stores studying the demography of an area and determining an appropriate trade area. In the early 1970s, a local development company, Westcor, began to specialize in acquiring large, appropriately located sites for regional centers well in advance of when department stores would be ready to build. They would often join with the real estate development subsidiary of a department store chain in order to build a mall. Westcor's first major development was Metrocenter, which opened in 1973 on the north Black Canyon Freeway.

Following the spectacularly successful opening of Metrocenter, the city's planning department sought a way to become a more active participant in planning for such major retail locations. Because of the huge sales tax receipts, a regional mall is very desirable to city government. The City of Phoenix needed to be sure that it held its ground in tax collections relative to neighboring suburbs. The goal was not to discourage malls, but rather to encourage and anticipate such development.

In early 1974, the Phoenix Planning Commission held a retreat to discuss how best to deal with the continued development of regional shopping locations and dispersed employment. The commission invited representatives of the shopping center industry, and Westcor paid for the gathering. Ultimately, the impropriety of a developer underwriting the retreat led to a minor scandal and the resignation of the commission's chairman.[10] However, the planning construct that emerged from the meeting was subsequently adopted. It has been part of the city's official growth policy ever since—the urban village concept. The city would be divided into villages, initially nine, each with a village core containing regional shopping and employment. Near the retail and employment would be multi-family housing. Surrounding this core would be a gradient of decreasing development intensity. Finally, near the edge of the village would be the lower-density single-family subdivisions. Each village was to be "relatively self-sufficient in providing living, working, and recreational opportunities for residents."[11]

In 1979 the city officially adopted an interim plan recognizing the villages and a longer-range plan called *Concept 2000*. Phoenix's official decision for the city to be multicentered has been widely examined. Tony Downs, in *New Visions for Metropolitan America*, recognizes Phoenix as one of the most fully realized visions of the multicentered network city due to its relatively weak downtown.[12] Joel Garreau similarly profiles the phenomenon in his book *Edge City*.[13]

Initially, the urban village plan was primarily useful in giving the City of Phoenix a rationale for additional regional shopping centers, such as Westcor's "Village of Paradise Valley." Proposed as a 1,216-acre development in 1974, it was to include not just a mall, but surrounding sites for major office employment, apartment complexes, a golf course, and single-family neighborhoods. The mall proved to be successful, but the fact that the "core" did not have nearby freeway access long prevented the planned employment from developing. Most of the sites designated for employment uses were ultimately replaced with other retail or multi-family uses.

The urban village plan also gave the city a means to organize the geographically large city into management units, allowing citizen input into planning decisions. Planning committees were appointed in 1980, with the charge that they guide the long-range planning for the villages. These village planning committees quickly became immersed in city and neighborhood politics of individual development proposals. In practice, they essentially became review panels for zoning cases and forums for increased public participation in growth and development decisions.

The reality of organizing the City of Phoenix into anything resembling a series of villages proved difficult to implement. For one thing, the efforts to make the existing parts of the metropolitan area fit the concept was a problem. Many of the village cores failed to become employment locations, or to develop any of the characteristics of a compact, pedestrian-friendly mini-downtown. The core area around 24th Street and Camelback Road did emerge as a high-end office location because of its proximity to expensive executive housing and the amenities of the nearby mountains, but this was a market reality and not because of its designation as a core. Most of the other cores tend to consist of a regional shopping center surrounded by a sea of surface parking, a few low-rise office buildings, and some nearby apartments.

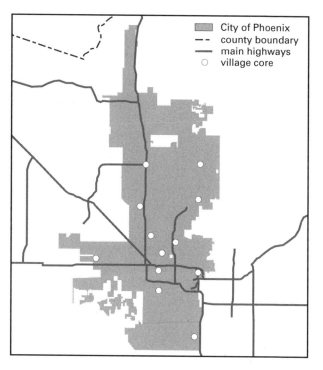

City of Phoenix village cores.
Source: City of Phoenix Planning Department

Another problem of implementing the new order on Phoenix's growth
was that most Phoenix residents often did not even realize they lived in an
urban village. The truth was they moved from one place to another without
any recognition of what was supposed to be their logical employment and
recreation pattern. In late 1986, years after the villages were designated, a
poll showed that less than a third of Phoenix residents were familiar with
the city's urban village concept. Only about one-fourth knew the name that
was given to their own village.[14] Travel patterns showed that residents were
commuting from one village to another for work, and they were spreading
their shopping around in varying patterns.

Prior to the advent of village cores, the City of Phoenix limited the area
outside of downtown in which high-rise office buildings (defined at that
time as anything taller than four stories) could be built to a corridor along
Central Avenue, from the downtown to Camelback Road. Even within that
area, proposals to build high-rises were typically met with great resistance
by nearby single-family homeowners. Many felt the buildings would loom
over their backyards, block their views of mountains, or would reflect so

much heat and light into their neighborhood as to lower their property values.[15] Tall buildings were an urban form many people had moved to Phoenix to escape, and having them nearby was not acceptable.

In 1980 a zoning application for an nine-story building known as Anchor Center, near 22nd Street and Camelback Road, was filed and ultimately approved after great controversy. This set a precedent for the city to allow tall buildings outside the Central Avenue corridor. A mid-rise zoning ordinance was subsequently designed to allow the village cores to accept taller and more dense office buildings to support the goals for further core development as employment centers. The mid-rise proposal, formulated by the Phoenix Metropolitan Chamber of Commerce, was intended to create an incentive for more intense employment development in the cores, so as to distinguish them from the typical lower-scale office buildings which could be built nearly anywhere on an arterial road. But if most residents of Phoenix were not aware they lived in a village, they had no idea that the "core" would someday have tall buildings, and such proposals were invariably met with massive neighborhood opposition. The village planning committees became the central focus for an emerging backlash against intense development. By the mid-1980s, a coalition of neighborhood groups was formed to share information about how to oppose such rezoning. Cases began to require a long public review process, which included hearings at the village committee, the planning commission, and the city council.

Largely as a result of personal efforts by Mayor Terry Goddard, the City of Phoenix refocused its efforts on the downtown core, beginning in the late 1980s. Voters approved a massive investment in new cultural facilities and additional city government buildings. The America West Arena resulted, and the City of Phoenix granted major tax incentives to both office and retail uses. By the late 1990s, Bank One Ballpark opened and Phoenix seemed finally to be getting a real downtown. Its focus was sports, entertainment, and government, rather than jobs and retail.

The debates about intensity of development in urban cores and about the role of downtown highlights the conflicted sense Phoenix residents have of their city. To Phoenicians, intense urban life is something to visit, whether in San Francisco, in downtown Phoenix, or anywhere else. But faced with a choice of where to live, most continue to opt for low-density single-family neighborhoods. Even many of the citizens who have chosen to be near Central Avenue or 24th Street and Camelback Road often oppose further intense development near them, no matter what the city's general plan may say. Greater residential density, increased commercial intensity, and building height are all threats to the perceived benefits of the single-family home lifestyle: a quiet street, a private backyard, independence from neighbors, distance from non-residential uses. No matter how much criticism is leveled at that lifestyle, residents are rarely interested in moving in the direction of more traditional "city life."

In hindsight, it seems almost ludicrous that anyone would have suggested that government guarantee the economic performance of an industry that it did not regulate. Of course, that is precisely what the U.S. Congress was persuaded to do in 1982. The federally insured mortgage and savings and loans companies had built post-war America. But the inflation of the 1970s meant that the savings and loans were paying high interest rates on their deposits, and loaning it out for home mortgages was a money-losing proposition. So in the deregulatory ethic of the era, the solution was to allow the savings and loans to invest in a wider variety of businesses.

In the world of Arizona real estate, savings and loan deregulation meant direct investments in development projects. No one figured out the system better than Charlie Keating. Keating had first moved to Phoenix in 1978, when he bought Continental Homes and turned it into the largest homebuilder in the state. In 1983 he bought Lincoln Savings in California for $51 million, and obtained a billion dollars worth of investment leverage. Keating used his ability to tap investors in California to funnel money into huge real estate projects, especially in the Phoenix area.[16] While Charlie Keating is the most infamous player in the overheated market of the mid-1980s, virtually every savings and loan in Arizona was caught up in a frenzy of real estate investment. The parent company of APS, Pinnacle West, bought the largest thrift, MeraBank, for $426 million in 1986. A venerable Arizona institution, Western Savings and Loan, made $581 million in real estate investments. For a short time, it seemed that the new entrepreneurial options for publicly insured money were a stroke of extraordinary good fortune for the Sunbelt, the final piece of the biggest boom ever.

In 1988, Barron's ran Jonathan Laing's now legendary piece on Phoenix.[17] The lengthy article chronicled the savings and loan industry's diversification into real estate. It also noted the rise of home foreclosures, mounting vacancies, and the downturn in migration, all of which pointed, in Laing's view, to a potential crash such as had been seen in other Western cities:

> In the end, Phoenix is proving to be as much a one-industry town as Houston or Denver, though the locals are only now waking up to that fact. The industry isn't oil, of course. It's growth. For if one totes up all the construction workers, real-estate brokers and syndicators, insurance salesmen, architects, appraisers, bankers and thrift operatives, and government employees directly involved in new construction, the number comes to nearly 20 percent of the work force. Likewise, growth, more than any other element, creates the illusion of prosperity in Maricopa

County. In actuality, per capita income in the Phoenix area has rarely matched and usually trails the national average for metropolitan areas.

Laing proved to be relatively accurate. During the first half of 1989, banks in Arizona lost more money than those in any other state.[18] MeraBank stopped all loans in July of 1989. Keating's holding company, American Continental, filed for bankruptcy and immediately thereafter the federal regulators seized Lincoln Savings—which became the biggest United States thrift failure of all. Three savings and loans, including Western, closed. By 1992, the federal government's Resolution Trust Corporation (RTC) was the largest real estate player in the state. The bubble burst. Brokers who had been making hundreds of thousands of dollars a year found themselves selling cars, and real estate lawyers had to go back to litigation. The press and the elected officials quit worrying about quality of life and went back to wanting to boom. This time, their wish was quickly granted. The market crash began to turn around beginning in 1993. At first development came slowly, since it was driven by demand instead of by money looking for a place to land. But even without the free-flowing lubrication of federally insured money, the boom that occurred in the national economy beginning in the mid-1990s energized Phoenix right back into a high growth cycle. From a high of 21,432 single-family permits in the Phoenix metropolitan statistical area (MSA) in 1988, the number had fallen by 50 percent to 12,950 in 1990. By 1996, the rebound was to 39,646, just short of an all-time high.

So here we are today: a community of restless transplants, drawn by sunshine, water, jobs, and affordable single-family homes. Living the low-density, ranch house, automobile-based dream of post-war America. From its earliest history, this community has been fixated on surviving and growing in the desert. Growing in order to capture water. Growing in order to compete with California. Growing in order to sell land. Growing in order to demonstrate that this is a great place. Once the growth engine finally got rolling, we didn't want to stop and think too much about what kind of growth, or where it should be, or how big we should get. The only self-image Phoenix ever developed was of growth. Well, we grew. Now what?

Agents So Commonplace

To Sprawl or Not to Sprawl

When Phoenix is compared to the cities of the world, it is invariably described as sprawling. Undeniably, the city covers a large geographic area. Professor Ignacio San Martin of the Arizona State University College of Architecture and Environmental Design likes to point out that the city limits of Phoenix could contain Paris, San Francisco, Rome, Manhattan, and Washington, D.C.[1] But city areas tell us more about the governmental jurisdiction than the form of the urbanized area—by this measure, the largest U.S. city is Jacksonville, Florida, because its city and county are combined into a single unit.[2] Ranked by population, Jacksonville is nineteenth.

Any meaningful comparison of urbanized areas is extremely difficult. How does one decide where the edge of urbanization is in a place as densely populated as northern Europe? How many urban areas are New York City, Newark, and Philadelphia? Definitions and line drawing are not consistent from one country to another, or even from one region to another. At least as to U.S. cities, the census gives us some standards to use for comparison. Tables 1, 2, and 3 suggest the deficiencies of using city limits as the standard for comparison. Even metropolitan area numbers are misleading, since metropolitan areas are often set by county lines. The Phoenix metropolitan area is sometimes defined as Maricopa County (9,300 square miles) or as Maricopa and Pinal Counties (15,000 square miles). The reality is that counties in Arizona do not work well for this purpose, since they are so large and consist mostly of empty desert. The "urbanized" portion of Maricopa and Pinal Counties today is about 1,500 square miles at most, with a population of about 3,000,000, suggesting an "urban" density of 2,000 per square mile, not a particularly low number.

The term urban sprawl was first popularized by William Whyte in 1958's *The Exploding Metropolis*.[3] It has since become one of the preeminent iconographic images of our day: a symbol of all that is wrong with modern America. Through the critiques of the New Urbanists, the diatribes of James Howard Kunstler, academic debates among planning professors, the coverage of popular media, the intercourse of chat rooms and web sites, the American public hears that sprawl is a wasteful, destructive, threatening development pattern that should be halted by whatever means possible.[4]

In its early usage, the term *urban sprawl* was an indictment of specific patterns of development, such as the commercial ribbons, or strips, along both sides of a highway where development was only one lot deep. A seminal 1962 article, Marion Clawson's "Urban Sprawl and Speculation in Suburban Land," examined the leapfrog nature of automobile-oriented growth.[5] Because the automobile allows almost any parcel to be easily

Table 1: City Limits			
City	Land Area (mi^2)	Population	Density (pop/mi^2)
Phoenix	419.9	983,403	2,342.0
New York City	308.9	7,322,564	23,705.3
San Francisco	46.7	723,959	15,502.3

Table 2: Metropolitan Areas			
Phoenix-Mesa	9,204.0	2,122,101	230.6
New York-Northern N.J.-Long Island	1,147.6	8,546,846	7,447.6
San Francisco-Oakland-San Jose	7,368.5	6,253,311	848.7

Table 3: Urbanized Areas			
Phoenix	741.1	2,006,239	2,707.1
New York-Northeastern N.J.	1,476.3	10,930,132	7,403.7
San Francisco-Oakland	874.1	3,629,516	4,152.3

Tables 1, 2, and 3 illustrate the difficulty in comparing density statistics across dissimilar urban areas. These are 1990 statistics, all drawn from the U.S. Census Bureau. Table 1 uses the frequently cited "city limits" comparison. By this measure, the large geographic jurisdiction of the City of Phoenix drives the comparable density very low compared with the more traditional San Francisco and New York City statistics. But such a comparison ignores the huge metropolitan populations in greater New York and the Bay Area that are in surrounding cities. Table 2 uses the census definition of metropolitan area. But these statistics are also skewed. By this measure, the Phoenix metropolitan area is defined as all of Maricopa County, a 9,000-square-mile jurisdiction, most of which is utterly vacant. The large counties and uninhabited mountainous portions of the Bay Area similarly drive its density to an unrealistically low number. Table 3 represents an effort to actually define the urbanized areas of these cities and compare densities. The Census Bureau uses a definition based on contiguous high-density census blocks to delineate these areas. Here, even these disparate urban agglomerations begin to converge.

Source: Bureau of the Census 1993a, 36, 40; 1993b, 69, 86; 1993c, 89, 97.

accessed, discontiguous parcels of land develop while adjacent parcels are skipped over and may remain long vacant. Clawson's criticisms of leapfrog development were directed at the inefficiencies of the resulting travel pattern and the fact that infrastructure investments are needed to serve the more remote parcels. Meanwhile, excess previously installed infrastructure cannot be amortized over the vacant infill parcels.

Today, the indictment of sprawl as a growth pattern goes far beyond the leapfrog nature of development into a much more systematic campaign against "low density, automobile-dependent development which occurs at the fringes of the urban landscape."[6] In older metropolitan areas, which grew to be big cities before the automobile was dominant, the auto-oriented "sprawl development" taking place today is seen as a threat to the existing fabric of the city, and especially to historic downtown cores. Between 1950 and 1990, metropolitan Philadelphia gained over a million residents, while the City of Philadelphia declined by half a million. The Cleveland metropolitan area expanded by a third while its population actually declined. Before 1950, central cities held most of the employment opportunities, and were themselves the most populous parts of a metropolitan area. In 1950, seven out of ten metropolitan area residents lived inside the main central city. Forty years later, only four out of ten were left. Employment also moved to the suburbs, either with or in advance of the people. By 1990, only half as many Americans made the traditional commute from suburb to city center as were traveling from home to workplace without ever leaving the suburbs.[7]

According to its critics, not only does this dispersion and deconcentration of population threaten the historic inner-city core of older American cities, it also threatens the surrounding small town and rural lifestyle. As the city itself disperses and spreads, the small towns that were originally economically independent are overrun by suburban growth that turns them into parasitic appendages of the city. Farmland is consumed and developed, often at relatively low residential densities of one or two units to the acre—shopping malls replace main streets, subdivisions replace farms. As cities become less dense, rural areas become more dense, converging toward the dreaded geography of nowhere.[8] It is this phenomenon that led the National Trust for Historic Preservation to put the entire state of Vermont on its "eleven most endangered places list" because small towns are disappearing with the onslaught of homogenized big box retail stores like Wal-Mart.

Sprawl is also blamed for gobbling up open space, farmland, and natural habitat; destroying historic battlefields, archeological sites, and significant cultural landscapes; degrading air quality, livability, and causing pollution; increasing crime, drug use, and social alienation by segregating population groups; and being financially ruinous because the capital cost of new infrastructure and the operating costs of low-density development are greater than with more compact urban forms.[9] Name an ill of modern American society, and the chances are someone has traced it to sprawl.

In many ways the charges being leveled at suburban and low-density growth patterns parallel criticisms made of the nineteenth-century industrial city. At the turn of the century, immigrant families were flooding into high-rise tenements with unsanitary and dangerous living conditions. The concentration of new waves of urban poor in badly built and high-density areas was seen as breeding social pathologies, high crime rates, and cluttered and filthy urban environments. The City Beautiful movement, the Columbian Exposition, early zoning ordinances, and Ebenezer Howard's Garden Cities of Tomorrow were all reactions to the high-density squalor of nineteenth-century urban form. These movements formed part of the impetus for changing the growth pattern of America into what was supposed to be a less dense, more bucolic existence.

Modern metropolitan areas are not the product of demons, fools, or conspiracies any more or any less than the industrial or pre-industrial city. City forms result from social and economic functions tending to gravitate where they operate efficiently.[10] Decentralization has been a significant factor in urban growth for a long time. The demands for large industrial plants made spreading big cities necessary, beginning in the late nineteenth century. At that time, both Philadelphia and Detroit were criticized for their large land areas. A key part of that early "sprawl" was that the retail districts in many city centers were fully built, and could not be readily expanded without wholesale demolition and replacement.

When the City Beautiful and the Garden City collided with the automobile, the rise of the middle class, the federal government's emphasis on home ownership, and migration to the West, large-scale "sprawl" was born. As Los Angeles planner and journalist Bill Fulton explains, "Though derided by Mumford and other Garden City leaders, the typical post-war suburb actually was an auto dominated derivation of their idea, complete with a neighborhood unit that insulated the interior residential streets from through traffic speeding along arterial routes lined with strip malls."[11]

To many of the critics of urban sprawl, the City of Phoenix is a veritable poster child for all that is wrong: a place where everyone owns a car, where most people live in detached single-family homes and shop in malls. An amorphous place of no place. Yet, measured against many of the classic evils of sprawl, metropolitan Phoenix fares relatively well.

First, it is impossible to make the case that the development of peripheral subdivisions and related commercial use on the edge of Phoenix threatens the city's core. When Phoenix began to boom on the edge in the 1950s, it had

A desert city tends to have a clean edge between development and vacant desert—the result of topography, pubic ownership, and infrastructure needs. North Scottsdale's edge is clearly visible from the air.
© Landiscor, Inc.

the downtown of a city of less than 100,000. The downtown stagnated as it spread out along Central Avenue, but it did not go from being the vibrant center of a major metropolitan area to becoming the deteriorated no-man's land like so many older American cities. In the late 1980s and early 1990s, when Phoenix continued to build on its edge at a prodigious rate, the downtown simultaneously experienced a remarkable renaissance. A May 1996 article in the real estate section of the *New York Times* noted that Phoenix had invested a billion dollars in downtown cultural and entertainment projects in a five-year period.[12] Over that same five years, metropolitan Phoenix probably added at least 50,000 new houses and apartments on the urban edge.

Similarly, the transformation of once independent small towns into bedroom communities and employment locations is not a sprawl phenomenon widely experienced in a desert city. Phoenix has few truly rural areas outside its borders. The residents of Cave Creek may like to call themselves "rural," but hardly any are farming or ranching for a living. The truth is, most of them are living a low-density suburban life, commuting to north

Scottsdale, Phoenix, or another suburb. Granted, there are large and important agricultural areas still remaining on the perimeter of Phoenix, and even a few small farming towns such as Avondale and Tolleson. However, the agricultural uses are essentially within urban boundaries, and the land is held in large ownership blocks, farmed by absentee and often corporate entities. Just beyond the farmland is vacant desert. To the south and east of the Phoenix metropolitan area, most of the farmland has already been subdivided, and houses run up to the desert edge. There are no rural enclaves of quaint little towns dotted on the desert of central Arizona that correspond to the pastoral landscapes of Maryland or Pennsylvania.

———————————————

Subdivision development in metropolitan Phoenix is relatively orderly and contiguous. The phenomenon of random subdivisions springing up five, ten, and fifteen miles outside the edge of the urban area is rare because desert development is only possible where the water delivery infrastructure can be tapped.[13] With the limitation on groundwater pumping now in effect, the infrastructure of water delivery confines the habitable area in central Arizona to a defined bubble. It is a pretty big bubble, but its outline is distinct. Metropolitan Phoenix has a cleaner edge than most American cities.

Of course, there is leapfrog development in the urban area, and many skipped-over parcels remain vacant for long periods of time. Central Phoenix, for example, has a very substantial number of vacant parcels awaiting some future development cycle.[14] But in examining the development of land in leapfrog patterns, Marion Clawson recognized that in a society of private property this phenomenon will always exist. Government cannot mandate when a given parcel will develop and has only limited power to encourage its timing. If a property owner wants to hold out in hopes of greater speculative values at a later point in time, there is little that a free democratic society can do. "[L]and speculation, sprawl, and intermingled idle land are all natural outgrowths of economic and institutional forces and not perversions of them. Instead of surprise and shock that these situations exist, we should expect them."[15]

Sprawl cannot be said to be threatening the historic buildings of the City of Phoenix. Even as growth was booming in the 1980s, the city launched one of the most ambitious historic preservation programs of any American city. Starting from zero in 1985, by 1996 the city had designated more than 4,500 historic structures—a full 40 percent of its eligible building stock, the highest percentage of any big city in the nation. Tempe and Glendale have also launched similar preservation programs. Most of what is being preserved are the twentieth-century subdivisions full of single-family bungalows, period revival cottages, and even ranch houses that would elsewhere be decried as sprawl. Even roadside architecture, shopping malls, and strip commercial buildings are being inventoried for potential future historic designation. In 1998, tens of thousands of Phoenix residents signed a petition asking that a 1966 movie palace be preserved. While they were unsuccessful, the sentiment expressed was not necessarily invalid: what others see as sprawl, we see as our heritage.[16]

The typical criticisms of sprawl often do not make sense in cities like Phoenix. Some commentators urge, for example, that the solution to sprawl is development around "nodes or village centers" with average residential densities as high as five or six units to the acre.[17] Amazingly, this definition of the supposed antidote to sprawl itself is almost a precise definition of Phoenix's urban form. The average developed density of Phoenix is about four units to the acre, and retail nodes tend to be sprinkled on a one-mile grid—making most houses within half a mile of one or more possible shopping locations.

If there is a city more guilty of sprawl than Phoenix, it is, of course, Los Angeles. While we think of Los Angeles as the prototype of the low-density automobile-oriented city, by some measures it has the highest gross population density among the 20 largest metropolitan regions in the U.S.—a density of 5,800 persons per square mile or 9.1 per acre. On a metropolitan basis, New York is slightly lower at 5,400 a square mile. Phoenix in 1990 was at 2,700 people a square mile, not that different from Seattle's 3,000, and considerably higher than Atlanta's 1,900.[18] Part of the reason for the misperception of Los Angeles is that so much of the region consists of uninhabited mountain and desert areas. Single-family home lot sizes in Los Angeles are extraordinarily small, just as they are in the newer parts of metropolitan Phoenix.

The urban pattern of Phoenix is unusual not for an especially low average density, but instead in its relatively narrow range of density. The difference between the way the rich and poor live in Phoenix is not great in terms of the amount of land each occupy. Almost everyone lives somewhere between two and six units to the acre. Very high density by Phoenix standards means 20 to 30 units to the acre. Low density means one to the acre in the exclusive suburb of Paradise Valley. Even the lowest income areas of South Phoenix are generally built out with 5 to 10 dwelling units to the acre.

The "sprawl" of cities like Philadelphia is quite different. Older central city areas were built at 50 to 100 or more units per acre. Those areas no longer attract residents at the rate of the fringe suburbs, which are often built at densities of less than one to the acre in formerly rural areas. This wide contrast of density has simply never existed in the Phoenix metropolitan area. High densities were never necessary to support an urban population, since the distance and range of access afforded by the automobile was already present when Phoenix became big. The very low densities never developed in great numbers because it is too expensive to develop the infrastructure needed for living in the desert. The automobile and the complexity of water delivery have acted as counterbalancing forces—one pushing out, the other in—resulting in a city of concentrated low-density form.

It is also important to realize that metropolitan Phoenix is not an urban area that is becoming less dense. In fact, the opposite is true. Because of increasing land costs, new subdivisions are being built at higher densities than historic neighborhoods. As infill parcels develop and more multi-family and commercial development takes place in inner-city areas, the overall density of the city will increase. Since 1960, Philadelphia's density has dropped from 16,000 persons per square mile to 11,500; Providence, Rhode Island, went from 11,500 to 8,700; Portland's dropped from 5,600 to 3,500. During that same period, and despite its huge growth rate, the City of Phoenix actually increased from 2,400 to 2,800 residents per square mile.[19]

In early 1998, a coalition led by the Sierra Club and the Arizona Center for the Public Interest began circulating an initiative petition proposing new statewide planning statutes mandating that all Arizona cities draw urban growth boundaries (UGBs) delimiting a predicted ten years worth of future growth. Each city's plan would then be put to a public vote, and, if passed, could thereafter only be amended by future public votes. The attempt to qualify for the ballot was dropped in early June 1998, the result of a looming deadline, inadequate signatures, the resolute opposition of the business community, and an alternative that was passed by the legislature in response to the threat of the initiative. However, the proponents vowed to return to the ballot in 2000.

Whether UGBs would be a useful tool for metropolitan Phoenix is far from clear. Even the advocates of a Phoenix UGB repeatedly stated that they were not trying to "limit" or even "control" growth.[20] The UGB, they said, would neither slow growth nor limit ultimate size. Rather, it was designed to "manage" growth by affecting the form and density of future development. The purported benefits of this particular management technique are said to be lessened congestion due to shortened travel distances, increased residential densities (making mass transit more efficient and curbing air pollution), increased efficiencies in use of infrastructure (saving public dollars), and a rebuilt sense of community because of lessened sprawl.

Portland, Oregon, which first enacted a UGB nearly 20 years ago, is cited as the symbol of the success of this planning tool.[21] The benefits of Portland's UGB have been hotly debated, but the boundary is still in effect, having been revised only slightly over its life. For all appearances, it enjoys general popularity. There are, however, a number of significant differences between Portland and Phoenix which suggest that this particular growth management technique may not be the best for our desert city.[22] Portland proper is a considerably more traditional American city than is Phoenix. Its industrial-era urban form includes a compact downtown surrounded by neighborhoods, with small farms and agricultural towns at the periphery.[23] Before instituting the UGB, the Portland metropolitan area had begun to experience the same suburban growth at the expense of the central city, as well as the loss of surrounding farmland and rural lifestyle from which many other regions have suffered. Creating a hard urban edge was a logical response to these problems.

It also is not clear if there is any major consensus to densify Phoenix further. Indeed, large numbers of citizens feel future growth should be less dense. The most bitter zoning and development battles in the Phoenix metropolitan area deal with increasing density, and many of the most criticized new developments are those with smaller lots and higher densities. Single-family homeowners steadfastly resist higher-density housing moving near them, particularly apartments, which are perceived to bring crime, transients, and blight to a neighborhood. UGBs are inherently a planning tool to force higher densities, as UGB advocates readily admit.[24] Unless Phoenix first reaches a community consensus about the virtues of higher densities, we should not leap at the tool of the UGB.[25]

Even if there were such a consensus for higher density, the existing form of greater Phoenix creates serious constraints. In very rough figures, about 1,000 square miles of greater Phoenix is currently urbanized at approximately 2,500 citizens per square mile. Vacant parcels and undevelopable land (mountain preserves, parks, floodplains) represent approximately 25 percent of the total acreage, so the areas actually developed probably represent a developed density of 3,000 to 3,500 people per square mile—about five and one-half per acre. Suppose we drew a UGB around the metropolitan area that allowed an additional 300 square miles to be urbanized. If that additional area then developed at much higher densities—say 8,000 persons per square mile—the area could accommodate another 2.5 million people. The result would be five million people in 1,300 square miles, or still fewer than 4,000 per square mile.

The point of this exercise is to emphasize that, unless we are willing to demolish most of our existing urban fabric, we cannot realistically use a UGB-like technique to force metropolitan Phoenix to transform into a different kind of city. The most we might accomplish is to push our density closer to that of Los Angeles (5,000 per square mile). This hardly works out to be a formula to decrease reliance on the automobile or to eliminate smog and traffic congestion.

One of Phoenix's great strengths has been housing affordability. In 1996, our median home sales price was about 89 percent of the national average, lower than any "competitive" Western city other than Dallas. On that same list of cities, Portland was one of the highest—35 percent higher than Phoenix. Portland fell from being ranked 55 in affordability in 1991 to 165 in 1997. In fairness, it is not clear that this difference is the result of the UGB, as Seattle, which did not have a UGB until 1994, also fell dramatically in affordability. It is probable, however, that if a Phoenix UGB were successful in constraining peripheral growth, it would significantly increase the price of raw desert land and limit the number of new houses being built on such land. This would affect both the price of homes and their availability. The fact that median home prices are low and entry-level buyers in Phoenix can buy a new house has always been a major component of business recruitment.

An additional problem, again unlike Portland, confronts those who would draw a line in the sand around Phoenix. The unfortunate reality is that the desert, beautiful though it is, has little economic value apart from development. Farming is development in a desert environment, and would be prohibited by a ban on extension of infrastructure beyond the boundary line. The desert, unlike timberland, bears no natural harvest, and in the Phoenix area generally has little mineral value. Even a low-impact dude ranch means development. In the desert, to draw a line beyond which development is prohibited is to draw a line at which property values drop off, essentially, to zero. The aesthetic benefits of owning beautiful desert are insufficient to insulate such line drawing from a Fifth Amendment takings challenge by the property owner.[26]

In *The Metropolitan Frontier*, urban historian Carl Abbott writes:
Over the last half century we have slowly come to realize that western cities can best be understood as characteristic products of twentieth century America. They seem incoherent if we try to fit them into the mold of Glasgow, Toronto, or Boston, for they lack the sense of closure that lies at the heart of European urban design. They are simple to read, however, if we see them as clear expressions of the new technologies of movement and communication. They cluster straightforwardly along their highways. Their residents are tied together by long distance networks of travel and communication. Their streets and houses tell how Americans have constructed their everyday lives in the postwar decades.[27]

In 1967, former Albuquerque mayor Robert Riley looked at the new cities of the Southwest, the places derided as formless non-cities. In Tucson, Las Vegas, Phoenix, and similar metropolitan areas, he found that there was a pattern: "It could be that what we are seeing emerging is the third major stage of urban development—a post industrial city as different from the industrial city as that city was from pre-industrial urban settlements."[28] Reyner Banham's *Los Angeles*, Robert Venturi et al.'s *Learning from Las Vegas*, and J. B. Jackson's *Discovering the Vernacular Landscape*, have attempted to make sense out of the multicentered, horizontal city. But their messages were often received as interesting celebrations of pop architecture rather than as serious examinations of the desirable shape of urban form.

The reality is that places like Phoenix are not characteristic of unplanned urban sprawl, as is too commonly alleged, but rather are the result of social forces and deliberate regulatory decisions. Those forces included not just the technology of the automobile, but also that of air conditioning and television. Affordable home mortgages were part of the creation of a huge middle class after the war. Satisfying the pent-up demand for single-family homes created the industry of mass housing production that built Phoenix as it exists today. City policies of annexation and zoning encouraged and reinforced the growth of single-family neighborhoods, and the marketplace responded. In 1982, Phoenix Mayor Margaret Hance summed up the result: "Some planners have reacted negatively to what they see as 'urban sprawl.' If that term is translated to 'compatible low-density neighborhoods' it explains one reason why we now have more than 800,000 residents."[29]

The term sprawl is evocative and catchy, but like most "I know it when I see it" labels, it is not really very useful. It is impossible to categorize city development as being either sprawl or non-sprawl. Further, it is unrealistic to assert that any particular forms of development are absolutely right or wrong. Why is it that the classic nineteenth-century intense urban core surrounded by multi-family housing tapering steadily off in density before hitting a transition line into "rural" is necessarily the way to live today? Making such value judgments about ways to build cities shows a misunderstanding of the most important lessons of city development. Cities are products of time, technology, climate, infrastructure, and investment decisions. Phoenix looks different than Philadelphia or Portland for reasons deeply rooted in its history. Dismissing the product of that history as "bad" is not useful in understanding how to think about or manage city growth.

That many of the evils most commonly attributed to sprawl are not, strictly speaking, applicable to Phoenix does not mean that Phoenix should be immune from criticism about how it is growing. What it means is that it is important to realize what Phoenix is: a different urban form, a product of the latter half of the twentieth century and of a desert location. A city of consistent, relatively low density. A city predominantly of single-family detached homes, built at between one and five units to the acre. A city of dispersed neighborhood shopping centers. A city of even more broadly dispersed regional shopping and employment, in which transportation patterns are a virtual Brownian motion like that caused by the molecules in a drop of water.

The real challenge that confronts us today is not how to radically alter the city we have, but how to sustain its viability. The question is not whether or not the city should sprawl, but rather how to accommodate all the different ways we as individuals will choose to live.

City by Choice —————

Two of the most extreme visions of ideal city form were conceived in Arizona. Frank Lloyd Wright's Broadacre City and Paolo Soleri's megastructure Arcologies both rise from the nearly blank canvas that is the Sonoran Desert, from a place with few apparent constraints, much natural beauty, and the clarity of vision made possible by isolation and dry air. As utopian visions of how to inhabit a place, these examples could hardly be more different. Broadacre City lies far out on the fringe of individual choice—the ultimate extrapolation of the Garden City, a rebellion against industry and a celebration of separation and dispersal. Soleri pushes the idea of squeezing humanity into dense cores to the opposite extreme: "an implosion of humanity into cylindrical megastructures over a mile high."[1]

Both visions were intended to be liberating. In the mid-1930s, Wright visualized Broadacre as an escape from the crowded traditional city in which a citizen was oppressed by forever paying rent to his landlord and being disconnected from nature, unable to raise any of his own foodstuffs. By spreading over the countryside at a density of one dwelling unit to the acre, town and country would merge together and individuals could attain personal dignity at home and at work.[2] His Broadacre vision evolved during the journey of his own professional life: from the crowded Chicago of the turn of the century, through Los Angeles in the 1920s, to Phoenix.[3]

Soleri came to Phoenix to study with Wright. As Wright's vision was distilled by what he saw in the Chicago of Sullivan and Adler, so Soleri's thought was formed by what he watched going "wrong" in the Valley of the Sun. The low-density form he saw evolving in the 1950s and 1960s was not a vision of harmonious existence within a pastoral landscape: it was one of bulldozing that which was natural and replacing it with a re-creation of a different place—the very place from which the new population was migrating. The dispersion being realized in the growth of the urban Southwest was not solving the problems of cities, but re-creating them in a different form: traffic jams, dirty air, wasted water, and scandalous consumption of land. His solution was a return to concentration with a vengeance—more density than ever before, packed into "arcologies." "The passenger liner is the closest ancestor of the arcology," he wrote, explaining that people should inhabit a compact, self-contained vessel, afloat in the sea of nature.[4]

Utopian visions are valuable to our understanding of cities. By pushing limits in search of the ideal, such a vision creates a filter through which to view reality. Yet, as formulas for development, the musings of visionaries seldom operate effectively. Part of the problem is that for a vision to be striking, it necessarily must ignore the constraints of the existing settlement patterns, fragmentations of ownership, and limitations of economic reality.

Frank Lloyd Wright's model of Broadacre City. Buildings—from single-story to high rise—are spread throughout the landscape. Large park-like areas are interspersed throughout.
Courtesy The Frank Lloyd Wright Archives, Scottsdale, Arizona.

Arcosanti, including ongoing construction, in 1993. The buildings are densely packed, creating a settlement small in area with a sharp edge, surrounded by vacant and agricultural land.
Photo: John Trotto
Cosanti Foundation

The most critical failure of utopian vision comes from a failure to recognize the power of personal choice as to how each of us wants to live.

Between the extremes of Broadacres and Arcologies lies America. One way to view the morphology of an urban area is by plotting the change in density from the central city outward to the fringe. Soleri's Arcology, on such a scale, would be a nearly perfect bar chart, with a vertical precipice of high density dropping off to open space. Broadacre City, the other extreme, would be a horizontal line of more uniform density of one to the acre covering the entire area being studied. Washington, D.C., and Los Angeles have been compared in similar graphs. Phoenix measured on this scale exists as a relatively flat line declining slightly toward the edge.

Graphic representations of urban areas in the United States, particularly in the West, would tell us that Wright's vision, as prophecy, was more right than wrong. While planning professors debate the preferable urban form, the power of individual choice continues to drive the evolution of cities. In 1958, Wright wrote:

> Unknown to most of our citizens this more natural city is already by native circumstances being forced upon us all. This city is happening now on the ground whereon we stand. Forced by circumstances we fail to recognize as advanced agents of decentralization, these agents are becoming so commonplace in our view that we fail to apprehend them.[5]

Wright anticipated the motels, gas stations, and convenience stores that today dot our landscape. Often overlooked is that Broadacre also included concentrations of more intense activity—even high-rise buildings scattered in the landscape. Phoenix may be the closest realization to his vision. Our city's density is four times that of Broadacre City, 2,500 people per square mile rather than around 600, but it is closer than nearly anywhere else as populated.[6] Phoenix is also a triumph of home ownership—at more than 65 percent it ranks among the highest of any large city in the world.[7] In the affordability of a single-family home, Phoenix continues to lead the major urban areas of the United States, approaching in part Wright's egalitarian ideal.

Metropolitan Phoenix fails to approach Broadacre, however, on a number of points. The cost of infrastructure to serve a city with a density of one per acre, particularly in the desert, would be prohibitively high. Coupled with land cost itself, the infrastructure requirements would push the average cost of housing in a Broadacre model beyond the reach of the common man Wright sought to satisfy. The one-per-acre areas of metropolitan Phoenix tend to be the high-end enclaves that can hardly be described as bastions of equality. In fact, while the "advanced agents of decentralization" have been at work, the forces of market reality have been pushing the density of new subdivisions in the Valley ever higher, in most newer parts of town toward five units to the acre. Nor has the automobile created the full measure of freedom that Wright hypothesized. Personal mobility gives us choices, but at high costs in time, air quality, and ease of travel.

Soleri's vision, on the other hand, seems to remain largely a permanent construction site of quirky ideas plunked down in a bleak landscape on the way to Flagstaff—an interesting place to stop once every few years to buy bells and think about lifestyle. Most visitors who do so drive away from Arcosanti with the words, "I'm glad we stopped, but I sure don't think I'd ever want to live that way." There lies the failure of Arcology to capture the future—the failure to animate the power of individual choice.

As the density and form of existing cities are products of the time in which they grew, so the future of cities will be the product of times yet to come. Phoenix is what it is because of the coincidence of an arid environment; a late population boom; the widespread use of the automobile, allowing employment and shopping to be dispersed; conscious government policies and personal preferences making a detached single-family home the dwelling of choice; manufacturing of high-value electronic goods easily shipped by truck or air; and consistent inviting sunshine managed by air conditioning.

That there are disadvantages to the low-density urban form that resulted from these factors is undeniable. There are strengths and weaknesses to any particular form, and examining alternatives is always an important exercise. But, ultimately, the form of cities will continue to change as technology alters work patterns, communication systems, and transportation needs. In thinking about the future of a city we need always to ask two questions. Ffirst, what are the implications of current growth and development patterns that we should try to influence to avoid undesirable results? Second, what future trends with implications for urban development should we anticipate?

This morning I started writing in an office at the ASU College of Architecture and Environmental Design. After several days of rain, it was warm and sunny outside and I felt stifled, locked in behind the plate glass. Now I'm sitting in my backyard next to the pool. It is not warm enough to swim, but the water is shimmering, the sun is bright, the sky clear. I can see the craggy outline of South Mountain, and I look up from the laptop computer periodically to scan my backyard for the weeds I should be pulling. Certainly, in Phoenix, this is the right way to work.

I have done this before, of course, even before I had a laptop. It was always easy to bring home a folder full of paper to read and mark up by hand. When really pressed, I would even write things out in longhand on a yellow pad. Even now, though I type on a laptop, my first drafts are generally dictated on little tapes to be transcribed in downtown Phoenix and loaded into a network server, from which I can pull up the text by "dialing in."

Today, I find I am increasingly annoyed when I have to drive a tape downtown, when dialing in on the computer does not work, or when I have to check multiple mailboxes—electronic and voice. I don't want to have to relocate where I am to get my work done. If I want to be by the pool, I am angry and inconvenienced when the act of making hard copies takes me elsewhere. Sometimes I want to keep working while sitting in the Coffee Plantation in downtown Tempe. A month closer to the heat of summer and my real preference would be a cabin in the mountains.

Technology has not yet brought me to nirvana—where I can simply and seamlessly work from wherever suits me. We're not quite there yet; not quite fully empowered by electronic freedom, but we grow closer every day. I can send emails to my law partners and clients, which they can retrieve whenever, and from wherever, they might wish. If the Internet had a better filtering and retrieval system, when I need data I might not ever have to physically visit the library. If Microsoft's ubiquitous products worked more consistently, I might not feel compelled to print a hard copy every time I finish a few pages. When voice recognition software really works, I won't need to take tapes downtown. One day I might even get one of those tiny little cameras to sit on top of the monitor so I can just dial up a face-to-face conference.

I've been practicing law for 22 years. It seems like a long time, but by most standards it is only about half of a full career. Yet when I started, carbon paper was barely obsolete, typewriters had no memories, and the "word processing department" consisted of two very bossy ladies with desk-sized machines that ran on big spools of paper punch tape. Before my generation of lawyers stops practicing, portability will make it commonplace to practice from poolside. I already know more than a dozen of my peers who have made such a transition. They work from home—or so they say, since the truth is we have no idea where they really are. Their support staff is home elsewhere—or so they say. These lawyers email documents about, then show up for meetings to hand over hard copies for signature at the end of a deal.

Lawyers are not alone in this. The economic nature of lawyers makes independence possible, and the fact that all we produce is paper puts us squarely in the front of the information age. But on the other hand, our business thrives on interpersonal relationships, on gauging trustworthiness evident in a firm handshake, a steady gaze, and an unwavering voice. We are not innovators, we are parasites. We are shaped by, and, in turn, shape the relationships that sustain a civilized society.

Lawyers have long been the prototypical downtown tenants. We needed to be near the courts and the seat of power; we wanted to cluster together for economies of interaction; our egos liked the views from tall buildings. Yet even 20 years ago, the legal community in Phoenix began to disperse.

First to North Central, five miles from downtown. Then to 24th Street and Camelback Road, to be closer to "executive housing." Then on to Scottsdale, and now to home offices. If lawyers, with their need to be the center of attention and their chokehold on the commerce of America, can disperse and link electronically, so can most every one else who works only with information.

William J. Mitchell, Dean of the School of Architecture and Planning at MIT, looks at the city of the future and sees a city of bits in which the information highway begins to change the nature of place.[8] Mitchell does not, like Wright or Soleri, offer us a design for his city, only musings on its potential. He asks that we recognize, as Wright said in the 1950s, that changes are now happening "on the ground whereon we stand." Indeed, signs are evident that our cities on wheels are becoming cities on the wire.

From the 1950s through the 1980s some of the more interesting architecture of our auto-dominated metropolitan area were the branch banks that stood in front of nearly every shopping center. Given plenty of money and a desire to make a statement, major local institutions built flying saucer knock-offs, mission revival cathedrals, and postmodern palaces, each with a drive-through catering to the automobile. Some institutions went for a consistent look, while others varied their design depending on context and location.

Starting in the mid-1970s, banks began experimenting with deposit-only machines located mainly in major employment centers—in the cafeteria or employee lounge. The original machines only took money in, and as a result were not all that successful. The true automated teller machine (ATM)—which was on-line and gave money out—made its earliest appearances in banks' own branches in the mid-1980s. The real revolution arrived with the realization that the machine could become the branch, and could be located anywhere from a street corner kiosk to the wall of the supermarket. Today, few new branches are being built, existing ones are being converted to other uses, and live bank tellers are a vanishing breed.

The transformation to electronic banking was relatively simple and swift, because money is fungible, compact, easily handled, and easily delivered. It is also indispensable, and the convenience of the ATM overcame psychological barriers to its use. The impact of computer communications on other aspects of retailing will take longer, but it is already possible to email a shopping list to the market and have your groceries delivered. The rise of catalog shopping is likely only a way station in retail's move onto the Internet.

The retail sector is one of the most dynamic and responsive in the economy, and a number of forces appear to be converging to transform the landscape of big box discount stores that so many urban observers are still railing against. Large high-volume discount stores are an efficient way of delivering mass-produced goods, including TV sets and computers, but so are catalogs and the Internet. There are signs that sales of big-ticket items may be better handled outside of conventional stores. New automobiles, with their standardization and warranties, may be next.

Even grocery shopping may be undergoing as profound a change as when Piggly Wiggly introduced the supermarket. The refrigerator/freezer combination freed the housewife from a daily visit to the market, leading to shopping centers with abundant parking for cars loaded with a week's worth of groceries. Today, fewer and fewer families have someone at home with the time to plan a weekly menu, and eating out has risen dramatically. More families visit the market to get dinner for that night—and they prefer fresh or partially prepared food over that miracle of the 1950s, the frozen dinner. The impact of this change on development patterns is not yet clear, but one can speculate that it actually means smaller markets with more take-out and specialty food.[9] The next step would be to place orders in advance, by email or phone, so that your order is ready when you stop by on the way home.

Until very recently, we had two clearly divided ways of communicating with one another. We could talk on the phone or meet face-to-face, allowing synchronous flow of information back and forth. Or we could communicate in written notes passed by mail, overnight delivery, or messenger services, allowing relatively slow, and therefore inefficient, asynchronous communications.[10] In the last few years have come voice mail and email, allowing more efficient asynchronous intercourse. More and more business, it turns out, can be well handled in asynchronous mode, which allows careful reflection and has the benefit (or risk) of leaving a trail. It is the social part of human interaction that most desires synchronous contact, and that socially synchronous contact, whether for work or pleasure, can be easily structured around multiple environments.

Employment is already undergoing the transformation of asynchronicity. In 1993 there were 6.6 million home telecommuters in the United States, a 20 percent increase over two years earlier. By 1997, the number was up to 9.5 million.[11] Obviously, certain forms of work do not lend themselves to staying at home or to locational freedom. In greater Phoenix, manufacturing, mining, and construction together employ about one-quarter of the workforce, and for the most part those employees must stay put for the foreseeable future. Of the remaining three-quarters, who are loosely categorized as being in "service industries," another 8 percent work in the hospitality industry. Restaurants and hotels will become more important, not less, as work requires less direct interface. The remainder of the economy is made up of retail, government and education, finance, insurance, real estate, and business services. A large portion of each of these sectors is potentially relocatable.[12]

Greater Phoenix is well positioned to participate in the electronic revolution of city life. Our telecommunications systems are excellent, and about to become better as the cable and telephone industries begin to battle for market share. In December 1995, Phoenix was ranked as the best city in the United States in which to start a home-based business, because of low start-up costs, access to information and markets, and Internet access and support.[13]

When the concept of telecommuting was first introduced, most people reacted negatively, envisioning an isolated existence where we would sit, probably in a bathrobe in a somewhat dingy former bedroom, punching a glowing terminal hour after hour, taking occasional breaks to feed the cat. The reality is that few people will ever spend all of their work time at home, and the new patterns of working will free us to work in different places— home, an office we visit regularly and share with others, a telecommuting center that may be jointly operated by a number of businesses, Starbucks, hotel conference centers. Face-to-face contact will not disappear, it will just take place in different patterns. The impact on urban form is not yet clearly predictable, but it is already underway. It likely means a tapering off in the need for huge office buildings (with their commensurately huge rents), and a continuing boom in restaurant business.

Economists Doug Henton and Kim Walesh have written about the role of clustered work and entertainment nodes in the emerging new information economy.[14] They see these "vital centers" of cities as directly related to the disintegration of large hierarchical organizations into looser, decentralized companies and clusters of entrepreneurs. Such centers promote the interaction and creativity on which the new economy thrives. Vital centers may be based in the traditional downtowns of large or small cities, or there may be new concentrations related to the natural environment or centered on an originally dominant workplace. Whatever their origin, they will be places promoting social interaction and chance encounters, and they will act as magnets in concentrating sociability.

The electronic revolution conceivably allows ever-greater deconcentration of urban populations. The Santa Fe Syndrome—where the CEO telecommutes from his hacienda, supervising his workers in Los Angeles, is only the sexiest manifestation. But unlike the automobile revolution that preceded it, the electronic revolution is largely permissive. With auto ownership came the need to store the car somewhere convenient and safe, leading to carports, garages, vast seas of well-lighted asphalt, and multilevel structures in dense urban cores. Weakening the glue of the workplace permits, but does not determine, dispersal. Theoretically, electronic replacements for transportation may enable living at higher concentrations where cars are altogether unnecessary. Eliminating the need for rush hour could free us to live in either Broadacre or Arcology.

If the city of the future will be freer from a form dictated by necessary physical movement, freer to find its shape, then it will truly become a place in which the city is ordered by how individuals want to live. Some will choose concentration, some dispersal. Points of intense activity are more likely to be oriented toward voluntary congregation such as entertainment rather than toward jobs. These new forces are already at work, already shaping the city about us, and they will act upon the low-density urban form of Phoenix at the same time as they act upon the intense concentration of San Francisco.

In the future, the challenge of city building may be qualitatively different as a result of these changes, but in the United States it will be met, as it always has been, principally by the dynamic reactions of the marketplace. In a nation founded on the concept of private property, no clarity of vision about the future allows us to implement that vision by fiat. All we can do is adjust our regulatory mechanisms, our public institutions, and our community investments in a way to nudge future physical development of cities in desirable directions.

Limits to Growth ━━━━━━━━━━━━

Aerial views of Phoenix emphasize both the city's isolation and its convenient proximity to the raw material of urbanization: vacant land. As *Newsweek* said, there is no apparent reason why a city like Phoenix, already the seventh largest in the nation, couldn't keep growing forever.[1] We have no seacoast, lake, river, impenetrable mountain range or canyon—not even an international border or state line to act as a barrier.

In most cities there are geographic constraints on city size and form. Even where horizontal growth can continue, it is usually constrained in some direction: up the coast, down the peninsula. But Phoenix not only jumped its river, we actually developed in the river—after we took the water out. When we bump into a small desert mountain, we jump over or around it, or even allow development to march partway up the sides. Even if we choose to keep undeveloped anything resembling a mountain or a major wash, the continued availability of flat developable desert seems nearly endless. As we hear so often, however, that desert is disappearing at the ominous rate of an acre an hour. The Goldwater Institute has done the math: Maricopa County as a whole is over 9,000 square miles. An acre an hour means that 13.68 square miles are being developed each year. The county will be "full" in about another 672 years.[2]

Of course, this is too simplistic an analysis. Land is the least fungible of all commodities. Its development potential depends on location, topography, ownership, and availability. These factors may combine to make a given piece of land undevelopable, or suitable only for limited purposes.

Like most of the West, a very high percentage of land in Maricopa County is held in public ownership—64 percent.[3] But that ownership pattern is a far cry from saying it will not be developed. For a long time, many citizens of the Valley of the Sun—not to mention the realtors who sold them lots—believed public land was synonymous with open space. Since 1981, state trust land (nearly 10 percent of the county) has been subject to sale and lease for development, and about 15,000 acres of the county have thus far been specifically planned for urban projects. Federal land, either held by the Bureau of Land Management or the U.S. Forest Service, may be acquired for possible development through exchanges. Even if we take only the private land and the state trust land, about 3,000 square miles are available for urbanization, with only about one-third being already developed. By that measure, metropolitan Phoenix could triple its population without increasing density, spilling over into an adjacent county, or building on any Forest Service or Indian land.

At the existing density of the City of Phoenix, the 3,000 square miles of land that is "simple" to develop could easily hold a population of eight million or more. As growth occurs, density increases, allowing for additional

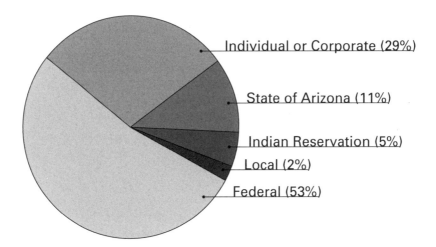

Land ownership in Maricopa County, 1995.
Source: Greater Phoenix Economic Council 1996, 64

millions. And the county line is not a realistic boundary, since we already spill well into Pinal County and are creeping into Yavapai. The reality is that readily available land in the Phoenix region could easily hold 10 to 15 million people or more.[4] So land is not a limit likely to force any change in the urban form of Phoenix.

Many people assume that the availability of water in the Southwest poses the serious constraint to urban growth, and in Las Vegas and other desert cities it well may. But in Phoenix, precisely because the search for reliable water has been such a major focus for decades of desert dwellers, water availability is not a meaningful (and certainly not an immediate) limit to population growth. A century ago it would have been. The serious joint efforts of our early farmers, boosters, and entrepreneurs created one of the most carefully managed and sophisticated water delivery systems in the world. Between SRP and CAP, Phoenix has access to very large quantities of surface water supplies that are both renewable and reliable. Based on those supplies alone, and at current rates of consumption, millions of additional urban residents could be accommodated.

Phoenix residents currently use about 250 gallons of water per capita per day (GPCD). This is a relatively high number, driven largely by the need to water acres of lawns and lush trees native to other climates. Albuquerque, a city that subsists almost entirely on groundwater, consumes only slightly less, around 225 GPCD. Tucson, another groundwater-based metropolitan

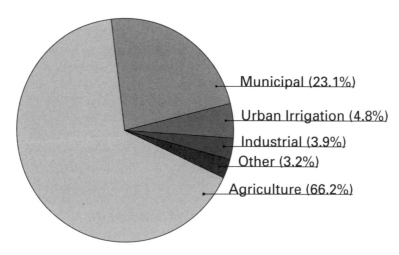

Maricopa County water use, 1990. By 1998 agriculture had dropped to 50 percent.
Source: Greater Phoenix Economic Council 1996, 64

area, has done a re-markable job of creating a conservation ethic and has ratcheted its use down to 176 GPCD.[5] The Phoenix/Tucson difference is both attitudinal and economic. Tucson has always regarded itself as a desert city and has little agricultural tradition. Tucson's greater elevation, milder climate, and more varied topography make its desert more lush and attractive than that around Phoenix. Phoenix, in contrast, was born of farming and has historically been an oasis.

The hydroeconomic difference between Arizona's two large urban areas is in water price. Phoenix sells retail water to customers at about $400 per acre-foot, one of the lowest rates in the United States. Tucson water costs nearly twice as much, the result of more expensive development costs because it had no great agricultural systems subsidized by federal dollars. Even Tucson's price is a bargain for water in the desert. Santa Fe and southern California residents pay $1,200 or more per acre-foot.

Phoenix's current consumption translates to a family of four or five using about one acre-foot per year. SRP alone can reliably deliver nearly a million acre-feet to the Phoenix metropolitan area every year from its watersheds in the mountains and forests of central Arizona. That water alone could support four to five million urban dwellers. The CAP can deliver another 1.5 million, but that supply is split between Maricopa, Pima, and Pinal Counties. Assuming two-thirds of it is available to Maricopa County,[6] that means another million acre-feet, and another four to five million potential urban dwellers. Beyond that, there are some other limited sources of surface water and some groundwater available at a "safe yield" condition (where withdrawals do not exceed recharge), which can support additional hundreds of

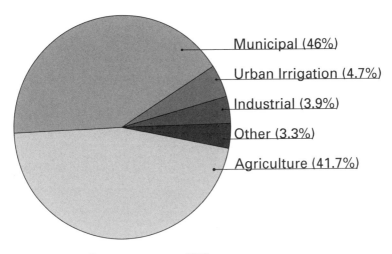

Municipal (46%)

Urban Irrigation (4.7%)

Industrial (3.9%)

Other (3.3%)

Agriculture (41.7%)

Projected Maricopa County water use, 2020.
Source: Greater Phoenix Economic Council 1996, 64

thousands of residents. Over time, even without any severe conservation measures, the fact that the urban area is becoming more dense, and that newer developments on the edge are incorporating more desert landscaping and water saving measures, means that the GPCD will likely decline.

The reality is that there are sufficient water supplies in the county to sustainably support a population in excess of ten million urban residents, almost four times the current population of the county. Few metropolitan areas in the United States could as readily identify available water supplies to support a quadrupled population. The Arizona Department of Water Resources projects that Maricopa County's demand for water will actually outstrip the supply at an earlier point, both in time and in population—somewhere around the year 2025, when the county population exceeds five million. Their projection, however, assumes agricultural use still in excess of 1.2 million acre-feet per year—nearly half the total demand.[7]

Water is not a serious constraint on population growth because urban uses will outbid agriculture for water when it is needed. In one set of projections, if the greater Phoenix population increases by 185 percent by the year 2025, water use will increase only 15 percent, with agricultural use declining 40 percent (but still using one-fifth of the supply).[8] In 1987 one critic said, "A simple shift from cotton farming to urban use could provide enough water in Phoenix to handle a population the size of New York's."[9]

If available water and land would allow the Phoenix metropolitan area to grow to a population of ten million or more, what other constraints might operate to limit growth? The most likely scenario is the lifestyle deterioration so many residents already perceive: brown air, traffic congestion, and

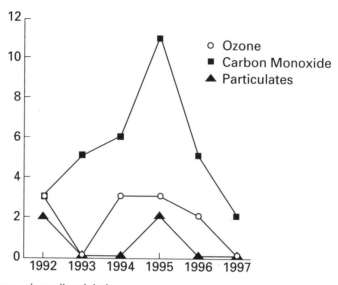

Phoenix-area air quality violations.
Source: Morrison Institute for Public Policy 1998a, 46

urban chaos combining to make a place driven by desirability no longer de-sirable. At that point, in-migration will begin to slow because the area is no longer a nice place to be—and, ultimately, deterioration will halt growth or the system will begin to correct itself by improving the negative factors.

In Phoenix, the most likely environmental limitation is air quality: all those cars driving all those miles at relatively slow speeds, inversion, and dust create the legendary brown cloud—and, by some measures, the second worst air in the country. The citizens of Maricopa County currently drive more than 60 million miles every day. On a per capita basis, Phoenicians are among the heaviest users of the automobile in the world. If current trends continue, by 2015, the cars in the Valley—which will significantly outnum-ber the people—will move more than 100 million miles each day.[10]

In 1995, the Valley experienced repeated air quality alerts, no-burn days on which wood burning fireplaces could not be used, and a pall of brown air.[11] While carbon monoxide concentrations have dramatically improved with emissions testing, ozone and particulates remain problematic, with the city rated as having "serious" air quality deficiencies by the Environmental Protection Agency for its failure to attain air quality goals. In 1997, the Phoenix area had no air pollution alerts, and 1998 was also without any of-ficial bad air days, thanks largely to El Niño.

Improving technology, newer cars, tougher emissions testing, cleaner fuels, and additional limitations on non-auto sources such as lawnmowers and leaf blowers may be able to keep carbon monoxide and ozone in a kind of uneasy check against population growth. Particulates remain seemingly intractable, however, largely dependent upon fluctuating weather and the dry dusty climate.

Survey after survey identifies air quality as one of the highest concerns among Valley residents.[12] National publicity about Phoenix seems to almost delight in pointing out the poor quality of the air. Bad air is a problem for any large American city, but especially so for Phoenix. Smog is particularly offensive in a place built primarily on the attractiveness of an outdoor lifestyle, deliberately marketed to health seekers and predicated on appreciating the sun. If sun, water, and land are the critical ingredients of Southwestern urban growth, sun may be the most threatened.

Deteriorating air quality is not the only form of weather modification that could become a limiting factor to growth in the Phoenix area. The Sonoran Desert, left alone, cools considerably at night even after a blistering summer day, creating a large swing in temperature within each 24-hour period. Irrigated agriculture altered this pattern, increasing humidity, and thus actually decreasing daytime ground temperatures.[13] Urbanization is changing the pattern yet again, creating a heat island effect, in which the average temperatures begin to rise since the pavement, buildings, and other thermal sinks of urban living do not quickly cool down.[14]

Old-time Valley residents joke about how it seems to get hotter every summer, but there may be a measure of truth in their banter. Statistics show that while the daily high temperatures are not increasing, nighttime lows are. It is hard to separate this factor from other long-term weather variables, but in the last 50 years, average summertime low temperatures in Phoenix have increased by seven degrees.[15] Arizona has the highest percentage of sunny days of any state in the United States: 81 percent. But this lovely sunshine makes Phoenix one of the hottest urban areas in the world.[16] Our city exists on the thin edge of habitability: if we continue to alter our climate, we may ultimately make it uninhabitable.[17]

Environmental degradation is a theoretical limiting factor for any major human concentration. There are precedents among great desert encampments of the past—when a nomadic band could pick up and move after the waters of the oasis went foul. The pure free-market theorist sees Adam Smith's invisible hand in this scenario. The environment deteriorates, people leave, and eventually a correction occurs—a balance between population and quality of life. But the losers in this marketplace are those of us who want to live in Phoenix, not just camp out here. Our environment is our commons, and as the tragedy of the commons holds, the village green may be hopelessly overgrazed to the point of uselessness because each citizen does not perceive the damage done by adding "just one more cow"—his own.[18] The negative externality of our individual decisions to drive alone in our own car or to burn in our own fireplace do not impact each of us severely enough to deter the behavior. When we all do it, we destroy the commons for everyone.

As a limiting factor, degrading the quality of the environment becomes a death spiral, because the quality is too far gone before incoming residents realize it and choose to go elsewhere. And as long as there are worse places to leave behind, new residents who are less fussy about the environment will keep moving in, further deteriorating the place for those who were here before. Sounds a lot like the last 40 years of history in Los Angeles. Must it be the next 40 for Phoenix?

Is there any way to get a handle on limits to the size of greater Phoenix? As a matter of setting an absolute limit, no. In our free-market democracy, no area can simply erect barriers to stop in-migration. Even the most draconian growth management schemes—those which ration building permits or create nearly immutable growth boundaries—do not purport to set a maximum population for an area. Rather, such proposals deal with either the rate or form of growth. To be constitutional, even limitations on rate, such as annual permit limits, must be based not on a theoretical "preferred" speed at which to grow, but rather on a genuine demonstration that the limit imposed is justified by the government's capacity to serve growth with utilities and infrastructure.[19]

While a hard limit cannot be set by fiat and legally justified, it is possible to create a "planning horizon" that recognizes a size manageable if properly planned for, and sustainable in the sense of anticipating a balance in which the lifestyle and attractions of the area may be preserved for an indefinite term. Developing such a population horizon for Maricopa County is a useful exercise. Having a projected population to plan against creates benchmarks. As the number is approached—if it is—adjustments in settlement patterns and lifestyles would become necessary. Having a projected optimal maximum also creates a reason to analyze the quality of growth—rather than simply to assume all growth is good.

For us, the easiest place to begin creating a population horizon is back at the source of our ability to grow: our water resources. Using water for such a purpose builds upon the one truly visionary piece of legislation we have in Arizona dealing with growth—the Groundwater Management Act. Unlike UGBs or other political boundaries, the use of water resources to project population limits has the benefit of being connected to real and historical limits and to the realities of desert life. MAG currently projects that the population of greater Phoenix in 2025 could reach nearly five million.[20] At current consumption rates, a population of five million would require more than 1.1 million acre-feet (MAF) of water—not a problem. SRP and CAP can easily meet that demand.[21]

Seldom do we think about water's fundamental relationship to growth and development. Instead, we treat the need for more water as a holy quest independent of land use, planning, and economic growth. Even the GMA's implementation has often led to silly results—like restrictions on fountains or incentives to replace turf with crushed granite. Such requirements have little real impact on water use, and only succeed in reinforcing the simplistic attitude that we do not have enough water, so we had better find more.

The outcry over settling the controversy between the federal government and Arizona by providing additional CAP water to central Arizona Indian tribes resulted from a fear that the tribes might control future growth in the state. Under the federal proposal, the CAP would be left with about 700,000 acre-feet for urban and non-Indian agriculture in its three counties. If Pima and Pinal got 200,000 of that, 500,000 would be left for Maricopa County. In fact, a significant amount of water allocated to tribes to settle their disputes is likely to be available for urban populations, but it will require dealing directly with Indian governments—something that some residents of urban Arizona fear.[22]

Regardless of whether the tribes get an increased CAP allocation, the ultimate question of water in central Arizona is the question of whether agriculture will survive. Water in the desert flows toward money, and that means toward urban areas. If we allocate based purely on economic utility, urban use will outbid agricultural use—Indian or non-Indian—and agriculture will slowly wither away.

Two recent reports assume, and even recommend, that the future of the West is exactly this—an inexorable movement of water resources away from agriculture and toward urban populations. A study by the Congressional Budget Office criticizes the past policies of the Bureau of Reclamation in "making the desert bloom" with agricultural favoritism at the expense of urban use.[23] A second widely publicized study by the Western Water Policy Review Advisory Commis-sion suggests accelerating a shift from farming and ranching toward the West's "urban archipelagos."[24] Indeed, such a shift has long been underway, despite the perceived political strength of ranching and farming interests. In 1960, agriculture consumed 86 percent of Western water, compared to 78 percent today.

In many parts of the West, particularly in California, agricultural and city interests have been historical enemies. The Imperial Valley—one of the richest farming areas in the world—has Colorado River water rights in excess of Arizona's entire entitlement. The rights were established early in the twentieth century, and are actually a higher priority than the rights of the cities of southern California represented by the Metropolitan Water District.

There and elsewhere, the idea that city water use is more important and should take water away from continued farming is controversial, and these reports lend weight to the urban side of the argument.

Arizona is considerably different. In Maricopa County, the farmland is the urbanizing area, and while farmers may feel nostalgic about the loss of their lifestyle to subdivisions, it is not in their economic interest to fight such a transition. The CAP was set up from the outset with municipal and industrial (M&I) water as a higher priority, and was based on a model of transition toward urban use. Because of these historical differences, we are today in a position to think differently about the water future. Instead of fighting on behalf of urban areas to pry water away from agriculture, we should be thinking about how to use water as a tool for planning the urban future.

It would be a mistake to allow agriculture in central Arizona to wither and die. Open space would disappear. Agriculture's cooling effects on the climate would stop. But most importantly, we would lose any connection to why people came here in the first place. From the Hohokam to Jack Swilling, the reason this place came to be was to farm, and it is a good place to do so. Preserving agriculture has to do with sustainability—not because we would ever grow enough crops here to supply the residents, but because sustainability comes from understanding, recognizing, and utilizing the resources of a place in shaping its settlement.

There are other urban areas that have made a deliberate decision that the pres-ervation of agriculture is important. Preferential tax assessments for farmland with dedicated conservation easements are an example.[25] Portland's UGB was in part motivated by a desire to preserve farmland. But in the desert, the critical limiting factor on agriculture is not land, but water. If we are to retain farming as part of the economy of central Arizona, we should do so by setting aside water for that purpose.

As part of trying to set a growth horizon for the Valley of the Sun, we should make a conscious choice to retain a meaningful measure of agricultural heritage by dedicating a large block of water to agricultural use with the assumption of perpetuity. At least 500,000 acre-feet of water could be built into our planning horizons as a permanent agricultural pool. This pool might include water allocated to Indian tribes and/or to non-Indian agriculture. It could be part CAP water, part SRP water, and it might include some groundwater. The water could be used in Maricopa or Pinal Counties. The important thing is that in modeling the future of the Phoenix metropolitan area, we should consistently reserve such a block for permanent agricultural use.

Allocating a large quantity of water to farming creates a limit on the water resources available to support an urban population. At the handy one acre-foot per family of five ratio, it would mean 2.5 million fewer people could be permanently supported. This suggests a population horizon for

Maricopa County of no more than seven million. We could grow beyond that, even with this water reservation, by effluent reuse, conservation measures, and altering development patterns. If it really became necessary at some point in the future, we could still choose to shift the water away from farming toward municipal use.[26]

Some of the controversy over CAP water use in Tucson represents a crude attempt to utilize water resources to force a limit on growth. The CAP canal was extended to Tucson in response to lobbying by business interests concerned for the city's future. An undercurrent in the opposition to the water's use is a hope that a threat to greater Tucson's assured water supply will discourage development. This notion is unlikely to succeed since it has been presented in a divisive series of public votes seeking to undermine current growth, rather than being more dispassionately considered as a future limit.

Rather than artificially constrain the amount of land available for urbanization, let us use the genuinely scarce commodity of our region—water—to project our future. To begin creating a vision for the future of Phoenix, we should start with the available water, remove a large block to sustain agriculture, and then estimate how many people might live here based on the remaining water resources. If that number is six or seven million, then our task is to envision a population of that size in this place, and to create a system to accommodate the growth that will take us from here to there.

A population horizon based on water supply limits is a radical planning notion. In many other parts of the world, there is a high likelihood that actual water shortages will emerge as a crisis in the coming decade.[27] By any reasonable measure, we currently enjoy abundant resources. But we must assume we will not get any new sources. Vast federal water projects are a thing of the past. Cooperation in establishing irrigation made this place possible, and cooperation in continued management of that resource is the key tool for thinking about future growth. Portland's planning tool was a line in the dirt. Ours should be a meter on the spigot.

Pieces of the Puzzle ━━━━━━━━━━━

Save the Desert ━━━━━━━━━━━━━━━

An acre an hour. It is not that Maricopa County may get full that makes this statistic resonate. It is what we are afraid of losing. The desert seems to be disappearing a subdivision at a time. The Sonoran Desert surrounding Phoenix is one of the most spectacular dry places on earth—not a wasteland of dunes and distance, but a rich ecosystem of majestic saguaros, intricately detailed pincushions, impossibly green creosote, scurrying families of quail, dinosaur-like roadrunners, pig-like peccaries, rattling snakes, and large bugs that appear to have been styled by designers from Italy. The most complex of the North American deserts, the Sonoran is a place we can approach, appreciate, love, and inhabit.

It is also a desert of some size. The first map attempting to delimit the Sonoran Desert as an ecosystem was published in 1911.[1] Since that time, most scholars have placed its size at about 120,000 square miles. Devoured at an acre an hour, the Sonoran Desert would survive for nearly 9,000 years.

Why then does the specter of the desert being consumed by development so trouble us? Part of the problem is that, in Phoenix, we were just beginning to appreciate the desert when we started bulldozing it for subdivisions. During most of the growth of the 1950s and 1960s, the city was still denying the desert in order to replicate a midwestern oasis. Even as the city grew into the outlying fringe, the new residents were reluctant to give up grass and green trees. Only in the last 10 to 12 years have we come to realize, partly through education and partly through government mandate, that xeriscapes could actually present an attractive appearance in our yards.

Most of our subdivision growth used to consume farmland. As the East Valley boomed and Phoenix, Tempe, Mesa, and Chandler began to grow, it was cotton fields that were being lost to subdivisions. Prior to the 1970s, the only significant "desert" development taking place was in the low-density high-end areas of Paradise Valley and Carefree, and in even lower density but less chichi spots like Cave Creek and New River. These areas were built a few houses at a time, with significant areas of desert usually preserved around each house. They were also places of greater elevation than most of the Valley of the Sun, with the corresponding lush desert. The small communities that evolved were predicated on living in the desert without transforming it.

The transition to subdividing the desert happened first in Scottsdale. With Phoenix to the west, the Salt River Indian Reservation to the east, and Tempe to the south, Scottsdale could only expand to the north. As growth moved north, the city initially adopted a policy of one-acre-minimum zoning. But when the available supply of traditional subdivision land to the south began to disappear, there was enormous pressure to rezone areas of the desert for production subdivisions.

At about the same time, the growth of Phoenix itself leaped over South Mountain. The first development there, called Ahwatukee, had been zoned in the county before being annexed by Phoenix. Ahwatukee first developed as a very ordinary subdivision targeted at a retirement population. Subsequent phases included larger custom home lots with horse privileges because the area seemed to be way out in the country. Subsequently, Mountain Park Ranch and the Foothills, two huge master-planned communities, wrapped around the backside of South Mountain Park. The Foothills had been the former proving ground for the International Harvester Corporation, and while it was beautiful desert with varied topography every bit as spectacular as Paradise Valley, much of it had been badly scarred when International Harvester tested its earth moving equipment there.

None of these developments caused a major outcry about the loss of desert open space, largely because the areas being developed had previously been unvisited. The public concern about losing the desert began when Phoenix and Scottsdale development leaped over the CAP Canal. For nearly ten years, the canal had been regarded, at least by the Phoenix Planning Department, as a kind of de facto urban growth boundary, a limit beyond which development should not occur prior to the year 2000.

Much of the Phoenix area's growth occurs at the edge, because people seek to be near the desert. The ability to access the desert quickly and easily attracts new residents, and the vacant desert mitigates the impact of relatively small lots within the developed areas. The desert is heavily used for recreation. People who move to the desert edge are often surprisingly naive about how long the edge will stay in place. When growth moves beyond where they landed, they become opponents to more houses just like their own. They remember a salesman promising them that the area beyond their neighborhood was not going to develop.

When the desert subdivisions first appeared, city planners and even developers made efforts to do a conscientious job of using desert landscaping to "preserve" the character of the area. With a new low-water plant list issued by the state's water resources department and mandated for public rights-of-way, and with an increasing sensitivity that water-gobbling turf and eucalyptus trees were politically incorrect, developers began to use paloverde, mesquite, boulders, and crushed granite in residential landscaping. Scottsdale was particularly active in mandating that large trees and plants native to development sites be transplanted and reused.

Despite such efforts, production housing subdivisions designed for flat farmland do not translate easily to desert topography. Both Phoenix and Scottsdale made efforts to use open washes to carry water runoff. But many desert washes are too shallow, and too ephemeral, to be very useful. Sheet flows across flat desert land and meandering small washes that move and

New homes march into the foothills of Ahwatukee.
Peter S. Morris

reform means that in a predeveloped state, water may be flowing across large areas of land. The dry exposed dirt of the desert is also capable of absorbing large amounts of water. But when development begins, the impervious streets, driveways, and roofs increase the volume of runoff. The lot lines and perimeter walls interrupt drainageways, and the water must be channeled to create predictable flow patterns covering less land.

Developing conventional subdivisions in a price range accessible to middle class buyers requires building at densities of more than one home per acre. Such a development pattern means, in turn, that individual lots are not large enough to retain their own runoff and must be graded to concentrate that flow in consistent collected locations. The result is that drainage requirements mandate altering the natural drainage of the desert through mass grading of an entire subdivision. The desert, therefore, can only survive in small pockets of leftover land, or be re-created in the miniature "designer deserts" of front yards.[2]

The desert needs room to communicate. A botanical garden front yard of cactus and sagebrush is attractive, but it has little to do with the real desert. The real desert is a vast, thorny, and wild place where the space between the plants may be more important than the plants themselves. Emptiness created by the absence of water as a natural phenomenon cannot be re-created on a 50-foot-wide lot fed by drip irrigation. It is the space between things—the "telling distance" that is the true communication of the desert, speaking of

The natural Sonoran Desert landscape, east of Mesa.
Peter S. Morris

Typical Phoenix-area desert landscaping.

dry loneliness and quiet separation.[3] To convincingly live in the desert requires proximity to the real thing. A thousand square feet of xeriscaping in the front yard of a subdivision tract home is to the desert like a goldfish pond is to the ocean: only a reminder.[4]

A prescient group of civic leaders in the early 1970s realized the importance of preserving the desert mountains of Phoenix. That effort also began with a threat to an icon: houses were climbing higher up Camelback, Phoenix's signature mountain. The city stepped in and bought most of the hump of the mountain above 1,800 feet. The citizens who rallied around the cry to save the mountain realized that natural features like Camelback Mountain gave Phoenix an unusual and important identity, a reminder of the place that we occupy. In 1973 the voters approved a $23.5 million bond issue to finance mountain preserve acquisition, and over the administrations of several successive Phoenix mayors, the city acquired more than 6,000 acres.

The nation's largest municipal park, 18,000-acre South Mountain Park, predated this effort, having been acquired in a series of transactions with the federal government beginning in 1924. It was not originally treated as part of a "preserve." In the late 1980s, a proposal to exchange private property for land within South Mountain Park where a public golf course would be built created a major controversy. This led to a citizen's initiative prohibiting the city from trading or leasing away any land in the mountain preserves and treating South Mountain Park as part of the Phoenix Mountain Preserves. From that point forward, the mountain preserves have consistently been cited as one of the principal points of identity in the metropolitan Phoenix area.

Subsequent to the original creation of the mountain preserves, the City of Phoenix has added bits and pieces by acquisition. Recently, a renewed push for open space preservation has begun in response to development pressures. In 1995, Scottsdale voted a tax to begin its own mountain preserve acquisition. In 1996, Governor Symington announced a proposal, the Arizona Preserve Initiative, to create a mechanism under which state trust land could become permanent open space. In early 1998, Mayor Skip Rimsza proposed that the City of Phoenix acquire 15,000 acres of state trust land in the north part of the city for a desert open space preserve. While a portion of this land was the type of mountain hillside that had previously been considered for the Phoenix Mountain Preserve, most of it is in low-lying washes that could be used as corridors of open space protecting the ability of native wildlife to survive in an urbanizing area. In the 1998 general election, the state's voters approved part of Governor Hull's "Growing Smarter" package, authorizing 20 million dollars per year of state funds be spent for 11 years, to be matched by local money and used for acquiring state trust land for preservation. A maximum of half the money may be spent in any one county in any single year, but greater Phoenix is certain to be the most significant beneficiary of the program.

All of these are important efforts to give metropolitan Phoenix character and quality. The most meaningful kind of urban open space in an urban desert environment is connected but dispersed throughout the community so that it can be routinely accessed both visually and physically. Dispersing open space has not only the beneficial psychological impact of reminding us that we live in a desert—and what that desert looks like—but it also breaks up the mass of development with large areas of temperature-moderating natural space.

As laudable as all of these efforts are, they still represent an inadequate piecemeal effort to address this issue. Not only does open space planning and preservation need to be comprehensive, integrated, and regional, the effort itself needs to capture the public's imagination. By the year 2020, the urbanized portion of Maricopa County will likely grow to about 3.5 million acres—65 percent more than in 1990. This projection includes areas actually developed, and areas within the development bubble that are preserved or considered physically undevelopable. Forty percent of the county (which has about 5.9 million acres), would still be outside the urbanized area, but this analysis illustrates the risk that, without comprehensive open space planning throughout the urban area, the accessibility of real desert to the citizens of the metropolitan area will seriously erode. The urban edge will move farther and farther away, making it more difficult for most people to reach and appreciate the desert.

Beginning in 1992, MAG developed a framework for a countywide open space plan. When it was adopted in 1995, the plan identified more than three million acres that should ultimately be treated as permanent desert open space of one status or another.[5] The plan did an excellent job of inventorying and prioritizing open space opportunities. It recognizes a realistic hierarchy of open space, much of which can be in private hands with conservation easements. Not all of the open space would be natural desert, but desert spaces are the priority for acquisition, preservation, and designation.

Unfortunately, like many MAG proposals, *Desert Spaces* is weaker in its proposed implementation. Four broad possibilities are suggested, ranging from the always popular "voluntary cooperation" among jurisdictions to a regional open space authority. No single alternative was advocated by the plan, and since its adoption in 1995, it appears that the choice by default is operating—voluntary cooperation by the multiple jurisdictions.

In less than three years, Maricopa County raised and spent nearly $240 million on a baseball stadium. We should accept the challenge to do more than that to save the desert. We should create the Maricopa County Regional

Open Space Authority, to focus on attainable goals of saving vast pieces of desert within our urban area. The authority should be given the power to acquire open space, even through condemnation of private property. The authority could contract with or assist any local jurisdiction in acquiring open space. Using *Desert Spaces* as a starting point, the authority should prioritize open space for outright acquisition, development rights transfer, conservation easements, and other mechanisms. Land should be targeted according to its environmental quality, but also based upon the likelihood of its development and its accessibility and connectivity. Much of the acreage in *Desert Spaces* is very remote from the urban area and frankly under little development pressure. To rally public support, the land involved needs to be close, visible, and reach the emotions of city dwellers—as the Phoenix Mountain Preserves do. The goal should be to permanently preserve at least an additional 250,000 acres of close-in open space, beyond the current efforts of Valley cities, over the next decade. This cause requires funding running into the billions, and a commitment of decades, but the resulting benefits are incalculable.

More than any other issue, open space preservation has the potential to be a unifying force for our sprawling oasis. More than any other element, our desert habitat is what makes greater Phoenix unique and gives it character and a quality of life worth living. Open space that crosses jurisdictional boundaries requires regional cooperation and creates regional focus and identity. We have been reluctant to empower regional government on any kind of global basis—unsure of what role it might have or what powers local cities might lose. MAG has too often fallen to being a whipping boy for road construction frustrations, while Maricopa County seems only known for running the jail and reporting on bad air. So let us use open space as the focus for a renewed emphasis on regionalism. Create a regional governance mechanism dealing with this single critically important and popular issue.

Desert space should become the hallmark that defines our city's efforts to cope with growth. It should be the accomplishment we cite when comparing our city with others. With commitment and focus, desert preservation can be the binding ethic of place, replacing the quest for water and determination to boom that brought us to this point.

Community as Commodity —————————

A sea of red tile roofs is poised to engulf us. My $125,000 castle looks just like yours. Our houses occupy narrow, deep lots, so what is visible from the street is the garage door. Your house, mine, and the rest of our neighborhood exist within a narrowly controlled band of acceptable colors: Almond Mocha, Baja Breeze, Hazy Sunset, Aged Tequila, Lariat.[1] In giving directions to visitors, we describe the color and model of the car parked in the drive, because only there can we find a distinguishing landmark.

Beginning in the late 1970s, changes in the cost of energy and construction worked a rapid revolution on the housing products being offered in metropolitan Phoenix. After the Arab oil embargo, the cost of energy began to climb and insulation became more important than ever before. It was easier to achieve high R-values in frame construction using 2 × 6s than with the ubiquitous concrete block. Steeper roof pitches also made room for more insulation. The earliest stick-built stucco houses were brought to the metropolitan area by California builders like Mission Viejo. At first, these seemed insubstantial in a market used to masonry. But in only a few years the perception began to change in response to advertising about energy efficiency and the increasing number of frame houses. By the early 1980s, a majority of new home construction was frame rather than block.[2]

Political attitude follows public acceptance. So, the neo-Mediterranean stucco with a tile roof quickly became the accepted measure of quality. One of the standard zoning stipulations imposed in residential subdivision approvals beginning in the early 1980s was that "all houses shall have full stucco exteriors and tile roofs." The ranch houses of the 1950s and early 1960s, in which Phoenix found its boom, would not be permitted today in most jurisdictions in the Valley. Car-ports, a composition shingle or crushed rock roof, and painted concrete block are now viewed as signs of cheap low-quality houses, despite the fact that many older neighborhoods survive just fine with these features.

The ratio between house size and lot size also changed rapidly. Nationwide, prosperous baby boomers coming of age have been demanding ever larger houses. Nationally, from the 1960s through the 1990s, the average size of a new home ballooned from 1,400 to 2,200 square feet, even as the average family shrank from 3.6 to 2.7.[3] Today, parents expect each child to have their own bedroom, a marked change in less than a generation.

The size of lots is driven largely by the increasing costs of public and private infrastructure. Builders seek to deliver houses at "price points" having strong market demand. One of the major components of growth in Phoenix has long been that new houses are affordable. The affordability of a brand-new home is especially attractive relative to California markets.[4]

Ahwatukee's sea of tile roofs extends for miles.

Entry-level homebuyers respond most directly to the question of how much home—in size—they can get for their money. So, delivering as much home as possible for the dollar at a relatively affordable price is the goal of the production builder.

Coincident with the increasing demand for larger houses, both the market-place and the regulatory jurisdictions began responding positively to "high amenity" neighborhoods: master-planned communities with fancy landscaped boulevards, common areas, pools, clubhouses, and bike paths. Cities began to insist on open space and amenities as a condition of approving new develop-ment. The standards of the infrastructure which cities required be built also became more demanding—streets needed to be wider and better built, sewer and water lines larger and more expensive. All these demands come at a price—a price to be paid by revenue from a development. The only way all those amenities can be paid for is to recoup them in the cost of home prices. To make that work, either houses get more expensive, lots get smaller, or both.

Since 1981, the average home in Phoenix has grown from 1,720 square feet to nearly 2,200 square feet. At the same time, lots have been getting smaller, shrinking from a minimum of 6,000 square feet to less than 5,000. As a result, in new subdivisions, two-story houses tend to predominate. A model home complex in the Valley in 1970 might have had one two-story model out of five. Today, the ratio is likely reversed.[5] Not only have lots been getting smaller, they have been getting much narrower. The smallest standard subdivision lot through the 1960s and 1970s was 60 feet wide by

A garagescape. With consistent setbacks, narrow lots, and only minor variations in design, color, and detail, there is little to differentiate these houses.

100 feet deep. As increasing costs of infrastructure and amenities were loaded on subdivisions, density had to be maintained or increased. To preserve the walled backyard with room for a pool, a critical element of the "Phoenix lifestyle," the depth of lots could not be decreased. Narrower lots mean that expensive street infrastructure is amortized over more houses, so lots shrink, generally in five-foot increments—in some instances to 40 feet or even less.

A small narrow lot, a relatively large house, and a two- or three-car garage combine to produce neighborhoods with a different feel than those of even ten years ago. Houses seem squeezed together by non-existent side yards. Garage doors, lined up to a mandated setback line, become the dominant feature of the streetscape. Front yards are shallower, with less grass. The combination of two-story houses and desert landscaping is often not harmonious. Mesquite and palo verde top out at around 25 feet, and even then seem overwhelmed by imposing rooflines. The homes do not disappear into the desert. Rather, the desert is covered by acres of concrete tile.

The images of garage doors and ubiquitous roofs have become emblems of perceived problems of neighborhoods that are bland, monotonous, and lacking in identity—visual focal points for every article on sprawl. Phoenix homebuilders say, "We build what the market wants." And indeed, year after year, buyers snap up every house they can afford without appearing to object that all of the houses look alike—from one builder to another, one area of town to another, one street to the next. Today, houses are commodities. Commodities produced by a relatively small number of builders. The five largest homebuilders in the Valley account for nearly one-third of the market.[6] Those builders produce large numbers of houses (over 2,000 for the largest) for a very active market.

New houses are commodities not just for the builders, but also for the homebuyers. Drive around a five-year-old neighborhood: there are as many for sale signs as there are petite oleander bushes. The constantly moving residents of metropolitan Phoenix buy houses not so much to live in as to resell. The smart move is to purchase a standard pattern designed to appeal to the greatest number of buyers. The lenders who approve prepackaged mortgages agree with this investment strategy, and prefer proven designs, emulating the pattern established by the FHA's practices to encourage standardization.

A perceived protection to resale value is strong CC&Rs—the covenants, conditions, and restrictions that are part of every new subdivision. These private regulatory provisions came into widespread use in the 1950s, largely at the behest of the FHA, which encouraged restrictions as a means of protecting long-term investment.[7] The most notorious CC&Rs restricted the racial makeup of buyers. Such limits are illegal today, but now we routinely regulate paint colors, additions, landscaping, and even the placement of basketball backboards and flagpoles. The intent is to keep neighborhoods as blandly homogeneous as when they were first built, so as to ensure the continuing viability of the houses as commodities. The result is that the neighborhoods themselves become commodities—consistent, predictable, uniform.

As our neighborhoods become commodities, so does the city. The forces of commoditization and uniformity have made Phoenix a great success in a world of growing cities. But increasingly the risk of that success is a recognition that subdivisions throughout the community may not fit together in an aesthetically desirable assemblage of neighborhoods.

The criticism of modern suburbs as monotonous and bland is certainly not unique to Phoenix. The rigid and controlled nature of suburbs and the development that takes place there is a pervasive criticism of modern development patterns. For example, in the early 1960s Lewis Mumford viewed the rush to the suburbs as flight from the unpleasant realities of life in a retreat to the bland and the banal.[8] Mumford was not alone. As soon as the trend toward suburbanization became clear, it attracted dramatic and relentless criticism.[9]

Today the neo-traditionalists tell us the problem is that suburban densities are too low; there are too many cul-de-sacs, walls, and entry monuments; that streets are too wide. Existing citizens on the edge of metropolitan Phoenix, on the other hand, oppose new developments because the densities are too high, there aren't enough cul-de-sacs or other "traffic calming devices," and there will be too much traffic for the streets. And both the pro-density and the anti-density advocates see government as the solution. Change the zoning regulations—that's the solution.

The appropriate role for government in regulating the appearance of neighborhoods is not a simple question. Any kind of government-operated design review system is a tricky business. Aesthetics enacted by committee tend to enforce blandness, not cure it. The dictates of legal due process require that acceptable behavior under a government regulatory scheme be communicated in advance and administered in a consistent and fair way. But the goal of consistent advance communication breeds design homogeneity.[10]

Even beyond the problems inherent in any government design regulation, reviewing single-family home design has additional issues. Major commercial buildings and multifamily complexes have an immediate visible impact on the public realm since they typically abut arterial streets and boulevards. Commercial buildings are visited by thousands of citizens every day. However, an individual house on a quiet residential street is primarily the business of its occupants. If they like it, who is the city to interfere? So what if people choose to live in bland monotonous neighborhoods—does that really reflect some serious defect in society? If there seems to be insufficient innovation in production housing, won't the invisible hand of the marketplace correct the problem eventually?

In 1991, the City of Phoenix had begun conducting design reviews on commercial and multi-family development. In 1996, the city government set out to tackle the question of government's appropriate role in regulating single-family home development. A number of elected officials were convinced that extending design review to single-family homes was a potential way of making the community look better and of heading off a growing anti-development movement. They charged a citizen's group, the Design Review Standards Committee (DRSC), with developing a way to meet their goals.

The DRSC was made up of architects, homebuilders, citizen activists, engineers, and attorneys who met over a two-year period in attempting to respond to the council's charge.[11] A broad range of philosophical views were presented, from suggestions by some city staff to review plans for every new house built, to pleas from homebuilders to leave the market alone. The DRSC was very reluctant to create a system in which a government bureaucrat or panel of experts would review every new home. The administrative burden would be immense and the risk of government-mandated design unacceptable. After a great deal of debate and study of building in the metropolitan area, the committee reached a general conclusion supporting only limited government intervention. They developed recommendations in three general areas. First, the design of public infrastructure has an enormous impact on the appearance of neighborhoods, and is inevitably the province of government. Second, it is appropriate for government to recognize and try to fix past problems created by its regulation. Third, if possible, regulatory structures should foster choice and variety, in the hope that individual buyers in the marketplace will respond.

The ubiquitous Phoenix-area house circa 1998—stucco exterior, tile roof, and a dominant garage.

An example of using public infrastructure solutions to improve neighborhood development included narrowing the city's mandatory residential street width from 40 to 28 feet, thereby hopefully decreasing the relative amount of pavement, and slowing down traffic. The city also chose to accept some variety in sidewalk and curb design by permitting detached sidewalks separated by a planting strip from a vertical curb, rather than requiring continuous rolled curb and attached sidewalk. Different street lighting standards, allowing shorter light poles in low density areas, have also been adopted. In new subdivisions in the desert, stormwater can be carried in open channels rather than storm sewers, replicating more natural wash patterns and becoming open space corridors. These changes should foster more variety in the appearance of different parts of the city.

In the second category—trying to fix some past problems created by regulation—the DRSC recognized that much of the narrow lot and garagescape problem in the City of Phoenix had resulted from an earlier change in the city's subdivision ordinance. That change had been intended to foster variety, by allowing options for development within each density category of the zoning ordinance. Previously in an R-1-6 subdivision, for example, all lots would have been required to be at least 6,000 square feet in size and at least 60 feet in width and 94 feet deep. Under the new options, lots would only have to average 6,000 square feet, and the minimum could be as narrow as 40 feet and as shallow as 60 feet. The result should have been a broader range of lot sizes with the same overall density. However, in calculating the average, a subdivider could include common area land used to hold storm-water run-off (retention areas). Developers could choose the average lot option without any review by the city, and the result was that most new subdivisions were built with large retention areas and much smaller lots. What had been intended to be a minimum size in a subdivision with a range of lot sizes became the average after the retention area was counted in.

The DRSC recommended changing the way the ordinance worked. Instead of being able to choose the average lot option without any city review, the DRSC's new proposal would limit builders to a conventional subdivision, with lots a minimum of 55 feet wide and a density limit lower than that which had been allowed under the average option.[12] A builder may select the conventional option "as of right" (meaning without any further city review). A builder unwilling to be subject to more vigorous city review might choose this path—which is, in a sense, a return to the ranch house lots of the 1960s. Under the proposed solution, the second available option, "planned residential development" (PRD), does not set any minimum lot sizes, and builders can obtain an increase in the density permitted in a subdivision—but as a tradeoff, the project is subject to city design review. The DRSC framework, therefore, rewards creative design but subjects it to the scrutiny of an aesthetic review process. This framework of options was adopted into ordinance by the Phoenix City Council effective May 1, 1998.[13]

The third philosophical conclusion of the DRSC was that government regulation could be used to foster choice in housing design. However, rather than mandating a particular procedure, the ordinance rewarded a decision to participate in the new design review process. If builders are interested enough in the "carrots" of varied lot sizes and density increases, then most new development will be driven into the PRD option and thereby become subject to design review.

The central dilemma in any design review system is how to provide clear and consistent direction without stifling creativity. Lawyers tend to push toward clear, concrete, measurable standards that prescribe, for example, the ratio between wall and window area, or the percentage of a lot width that can be occupied by a garage door. Developers will also frequently complain to a city engaging in design review, "Just tell me what you want," so as to move as quickly through the process as possible. Clear, prescriptive, and easily administered standards, however, can lead to uniformity—exactly what the DRSC was told to fix.

Previously, the City of Phoenix had tried to deal with this dilemma by using a design review system that stated objective standards but allowed deviations from the standards subject to approval by a review board. This approach was designed to meet legal due process requirements while still permitting flexibility. It also confines the discretion of the review body to selected circumstances. This system was adopted for commercial and multi-family projects starting in December 1990.[14] The design standards were organized into a hierarchy of guidelines called requirements, presumptions, and considerations. A requirement is a design standard that must be followed in order to re-ceive city approval. A consideration is something the owner or designer is encouraged to follow, but non-compliance is not grounds for rejection. Between the two fall presumptions, representing design elements that should be incorporated into a project. A presumption can be waived, but it is up to the applicant to demonstrate to city staff why it is inappropriate or does not apply to the project in question. If a presumption is not followed or overcome in a manner satisfactory to the staff, it can be appealed to a review board.[15]

Now this approach will be incorporated under the PRD option to include, for example, presumptions that houses on a street should have varied setbacks and side yard separations. The visual impact of garages must be reduced by bringing part of the house forward of the garage, by providing some side-entry garages, or by setting one bay of a garage at a different setback. As to individual home design, a variety of colors, exterior materials, roof forms, window shapes, and design details must be offered for each model. Visible front entries, front porches, or patios are also encouraged. By providing a number of these features, a homebuilder can obtain design review approval and increase the density of the project.

The Phoenix design review process has only recently been applied to single-family homes. It is impossible, therefore, to measure whether it will be successful in achieving the goals of additional diversity and character in single-family home development. Aesthetic regulation is tricky at best, fraught with the risk of unintended consequences. Single-family homebuyers often purchase new homes based on the interior layout, the size of home they can get for their money, and the orientation of the backyard, with little thought given to the appearance of the neighborhood once it is built. It is beneficial for the city to carefully craft regulations encouraging neighborhoods that will hold up well over time, just as it tries to ensure that the infrastructure will similarly hold up.

The single-family home is the most basic building block of the American community. After World War II, to own that home became the defining goal of the American middle class, as it remains to this day. It is a goal that is becoming steadily more difficult to achieve, even in Arizona. In 1990, Arizona's median household income was $27,500, and the median house cost about $80,000. By 1996, the median home price had jumped 50 percent, to $118,000, while household income rose to only $31,600.[16]

Preserving the single-family home as an obtainable goal for most citizens is an important component in the continuing validity of the American Dream. Larger lots, fancier materials, more varied designs, higher construction quality, more creative landscaping, neighborhood amenities, more rigorous government regulation—these things all come at a price.

The sale of houses takes place in a vital and genuine market. Like any market, better products at a better price will be rewarded. Like with any consumer commodity, tastes will change over time. The bungalows of the 1920s gave way to the ranches of the 1950s. Conversation pits and shag carpet gave way to media centers and walled courtyards.[17] The newest subdivisions in the Valley of the Sun already show signs that the infatuation with beige stucco and red tile is maturing. More colors and variety in exterior materials is evident.

Despite the dynamics of the marketplace, however, there is a role for government in single-family homebuilding beyond just ensuring that the houses will not fall down. Houses are a consumer commodity unlike any other precisely because they are also the building blocks of our communities. Long after the first buyers have moved on to a bigger house or a different city, the house they built remains a piece of a neighborhood. All of society has an interest in that piece because we have invested in it—in building the connections and infrastructure of our cities.

It should not be the role of government to interfere unduly with the choices individuals make in how they live. But the character, quality, and prices of homes that are built has been inextricably tied to government policies in the last half of this century, and will remain so into the future. We should constantly think about the impact of government policies on the way people are able to live, and move carefully in structuring the regulations dealing with homebuilding. The City of Phoenix tried to do this in the DRSC process, and the resulting system is instructive for other communities.

A number of other Valley cities, faced with angry citizens at zoning hearings and city council members critical of newer neighborhoods, have simply decided to mandate larger lots. The effect is certainly to increase the prices of houses, which in some places is an intended corollary—a conscious intent to exclude certain classes of citizens. Even where an exclusionary result is unintentional it is inappropriate. In contrast, the new City of Phoenix system allows smaller and narrower lots to be built but recognizes that at these higher densities the relationships between the individual houses are critical to the character of the neighborhoods that are created. Those relationships are an appropriate role for regulation.

Single-family design review should not be an open-ended standardless review by a board of appointed experts who get to say what they like or don't like. That kind of vague process, often created by private CC&Rs, it is not acceptable for government action. Instead, municipal design review should be a structured, professional process with clear guidelines and written philosophical goals. The process should include incentives for greater density and development flexibility if design goals are met.

Finally, it is important that cities with areas of different character (for example, building in the desert versus development on infill parcels) recognize those differences in the development standards that are applied. The standards for public infrastructure as well as for private development should vary in different parts of town. Infill parcels should be developed within the historic design context of surrounding areas. Subdivisions taking the place of flat farmland should have different design standards from subdivisions in the desert.

We should strive to maintain the single-family home as an obtainable goal while making our community more than a commodity.

February 25, 1983. The auditorium is packed with developers, brokers, reporters, lawyers, and curiosity seekers. On behalf of the schoolchildren of Arizona, the state is about to auction 190 acres of state trust land—medium- and high-density zoned residential land in north Scottsdale, one of the hottest real estate markets in the country. The auctioneer opens the bidding at the appraised value of $4.7 million for a sale at 10 percent down. Suntanned developers wearing Gucci loafers and Rolex watches hold up their bid numbers. As tension builds, the price is driven up to $5.5 million before the gavel falls. Arizona's schoolchildren have made a tidy profit on the property they had held since statehood.[1]

In 1981, Governor Bruce Babbitt signed into law the Urban Lands Act after years of legislative debate over the management of vast property located near urban growth centers held "in trust" by the State of Arizona. Statewide, 9.5 million acres are held in the state land trust. Only 18 percent of Arizona is private land, while 13 percent is state trust land. The balance is a mixture of Indian reservations and federal land. The trust holds almost 10 percent of Maricopa County.

State trust lands stem from the Northwest Ordinance, passed by Congress in 1787. The federal government gave the lands to the states for specific purposes, in most cases for the benefit of public education. The lands have fared differently in different states. Nevada auctioned off most of its land shortly after achieving statehood. New Mexico and Texas earn substantial revenue from their lands because of oil and gas revenues.

In the early 1980s, the state of Arizona concluded that its trust holdings could become a financial bonanza if the state got into the development business. A task force appointed by the governor identified more than 500,000 acres of land having urban development potential and proposed that new legislation be passed to allow this property to be released to the private sector.

The Urban Lands Act was a complex series of compromises, creating a system allowing the state to dispose of trust land either by sale or long-term lease after a cooperative planning process giving local jurisdictions some input.[2] The basic presumption was that any land planned for single-family residential purposes could be sold while commercial land or multi-family residential land for rental complexes would be put under long-term lease. Auctions would take place after the land was planned and zoned, either by the state or by a potential buyer acting on the state's behalf under a "planning permit."

In 1983, the first auction was held with great anticipation and considerable success, but since that time the Urban Lands Act has been almost continuously mired in controversy, often paralyzing the land department's decision making. The department has been castigated for disposing of land too early and too cheaply; criticized for not preserving enough land as open space; accused of furthering sprawl and low-quality development; blamed for not being aggressive enough to cash in on the real estate boom and help schoolchildren; investigated for being too cozy with developers; been boycotted as "impossible to deal with" by many developers; been touted as an economic development tool for the state; been blamed for being too eager to help land a major employer without considering environmental issues. It has often seemed that the department could do nothing right.

The Urban Lands Act was based on the assumption that planning and zoning of state land in advance of disposition would enhance its value. The goal was to receive "retail" value for the land—that is, not to sell too early in order to take advantage of the increase in price that comes after planning but just before development. There was, however, no provision for the state to install infrastructure serving the land—which is the basic transforming act from wholesale into retail.

The act contained another enormously controversial provision: a preferential right to existing lessees. For years the state had been leasing parcels of trust land on renewable short-term leases to ranchers and, in some cases, to land speculators. These lessees felt they had a vested interest and that their rights should be recognized in some way, even when the land was auctioned. The compromise was that if a parcel was being auctioned for a long-term lease, the existing lessee would have the right to match the high bid received at auction. Initially, this "preference" was viewed by the department as a commodity of great value, to be used to entice developers into dealing with the complicated and bureaucratic development process, since it could provide them with a leg up on other bidders.[3]

In the years immediately following the Urban Lands Act, overall revenues to the state trust increased dramatically, as did the size of the trust's permanent fund. Between 1981 and 1989, the planning permit and preferential right mechanisms were used to lure the private sector into spending nearly six million dollars for planning almost 20,000 acres. The state spent $600,000 of its own money to plan an additional 5,000 acres.[4] Criticism began to mount, however, because very few of the auctions had competitive bidding. A number of critics believed that the existence of the preferential right discouraged bidding. In 1989, in response to press and public scrutiny of the preference's operation and a lawsuit, the legislature modified the preference, hoping to encourage more spirited bidding.[5]

By the late 1980s, real estate developers and private sector consultants were becoming comfortable in dealing with the State Land Department. There was a brief but encouraging history of cooperative planning and property being disposed of by auction. But just as the process seemed likely to

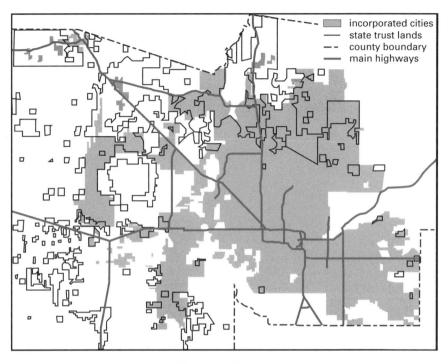

	incorporated cities
	state trust lands
	county boundary
	main highways

State trust lands and urbanized Maricopa County.
Source: Arizona State Land Department

settle into a predictable routine, the urban lands development program began
to come under assault from a variety of sources. Competing owners of private property were disgruntled about being in competition with the state.
The state's vast holdings in the north part of the City of Phoenix dwarfed
the available private property, and many owners were concerned that the
state could flood the market. The press also criticized the department for its
sales program. The department was in the position of marketing very large
tracts of property so developers could purchase or lease enough land to justify extending infrastructure into a new area, but when it sold large tracts of
property, it received what appeared to be low land values. After the developers installed infrastructure, they were often able to resell the same land
for much higher values. The press compared the two prices without really
understanding the investment required and risks of the development process,
and created a public perception that the land department was being fleeced.

At the same time the land department was being criticized for not selling
land for enough money, it was criticized for contributing to urban sprawl by
developing what was thought of as open space. In large part, this criticism
arose out of a fundamental misunderstanding about the mandate of the land

department. The Arizona Supreme Court made this clear: "The Enabling Act does not allow Trust lands to be used for the purpose of subsidizing public programs no matter how meritorious the programs."[6] The land department was willing to work with local jurisdictions to incorporate reasonable open space in its projects, but was not willing to go any farther than would a private property owner.

In 1986, in response to some of these criticisms, the land department shifted the emphasis of its program. The department felt that it could better manage more discrete parcels of land with infrastructure in place. On such parcels, it would not be required to install infrastructure but could immediately auction, for example, a long-term lease to a commercial developer at "retail" values. The way to get such parcels, the department believed, was to exchange large tracts it held on a city perimeter for smaller, more manageable, high-value parcels. In 1986, the department exchanged 3,000 acres on the fringe of the development area north of Tucson for 30 acres of infill commercial land. The transaction was based on independent appraisals but the department was heavily criticized for trading a huge parcel for a small one—evidence of having been conned once again. In the late 1980s, a new land commissioner instituted a policy prohibiting such exchanges and subsequently both the attorney general and the Arizona Supreme Court ruled that exchanges were unconstitutional.[7] Exchanges engendered so much criticism and public distrust that even though the department had engaged in a program of exchanges with public entities and ranchers for 50 years or more, the people of Arizona have three times refused to amend the constitution to allow the land department to again trade land.

After the department stopped exchanging, it was still faced with the problem of installing infrastructure to its vast tracts. The next idea was to work with a master developer who would install infrastructure to serve an area larger than what he would actually seek to develop. Then the department could sell surrounding parcels within the area at higher prices because the developer had brought in the utilities.

In the early 1990s, the land department was able to use this formula to successfully structure the disposition of the Desert Ridge Master Planned Community in north Phoenix. There, the department auctioned about 550 acres under commercial lease for an urban village core, resort site, and adjacent golf course. At the same time, it sold 780 acres of trust land for residential development with another golf course. All together, these dispositions were designed to commence development of a 5,700-acre master planned community. The plan contained a number of innovative provisions, including wash corridors acting as open space connections through the desert, an attempt to contain all commercial development within a single village core rather than dispersing it along the arterial streets, and a number of design

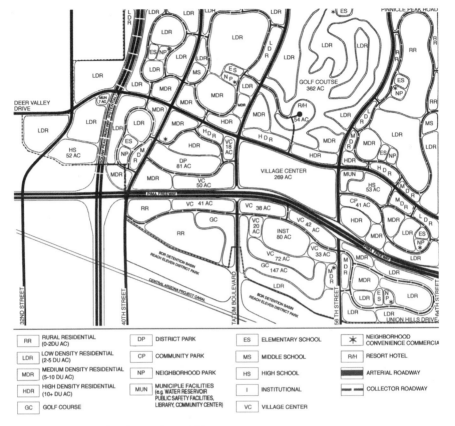

The Desert Ridge land use plan, 1996.
Northeast Phoenix Partners

guidelines and restrictions to give the community a desert character. At the time, Desert Ridge was widely hailed as the first real effort to implement Phoenix's urban village plan in a new part of the city and a model for dealing with the department's vast holdings.

Once again, there were complaints about the disposition. The initial 780-acre sale of residential land and golf course property was made at an appraised value of $12,000 an acre, with the requirement that the developer install very extensive infrastructure, effectively bringing his basis in the property closer to $75,000 an acre. But when the land was resold to homebuilders at approximately $85,000 an acre, it looked to the press and even to the Arizona auditor general's office as though the developer had somehow made a huge "windfall" profit.

Stung by public criticism, the department retrenched again, concluding that rather than work with master developers on large planned communities, it should sell smaller parcels directly to homebuilders. In a series of attempts to do so in the late 1990s, the department found that it was offering land to a hot market but receiving no bids because individual homebuilders were unwilling to deal with the problems created by a lack of infrastructure and entitlement uncertainties.

In January 1996, the department was ordered to cease all planning on a vast area of trust land in north Scottsdale by Governor Symington as part of his efforts to create the Arizona Preserve Initiative. The result was yet another 180-degree turn: from formally classifying the land as suitable for planning in 1993, to classifying all planning on the same land as being inappropriate in 1996.

The State of Arizona is on the verge of squandering one of its greatest assets. Constant political interference, bureaucratic indecision, and an ever-changing view of the role of trust lands have resulted in false starts, a climate of suspicion, revenues to education that fall far short of what is possible, and not nearly enough truly innovative planning and development. The problems are so serious and persistent that a complete reworking of the functioning of the State Land Department is necessary.

The department must be restructured to insulate it as much as possible from the political pressures of the governor's office and the state legislature, and to create consistent behavior that can survive a single commissioner or administration. The department should be managed by a board of five regents or trustees appointed by the governor for staggered six-year terms and removable only for malfeasance. The trustees would hire the state land commissioner, who would hire the rest of the staff.[8]

As part of the restructuring, a transition should be made to a point at which the department becomes self sustaining, with revenues from state lands supporting the department's activities. The activities should be subject to oversight by the auditor general and the legislature, but the goal would be to move the department entirely away from general fund appropriations. The department's personnel should be removed from the state's civil service system, and the department treated as a quasi-public authority. This means that department employees could be compensated on a system of pay-for-performance, rewarding their work in assisting the department to meet its mandates. This change is necessary if we are to expect land department employees to deal productively with the private real estate sector.

The Arizona Constitution should be amended to allow exchanges of state trust land, but only with other public entities. Voters have repeatedly turned down full exchange authority, distrusting the ability of the department to deal with proposed real estate swaps. Exchanges took place for more than

60 years before they became controversial, however, and have great value as an asset management tool. They can be used to expedite open space preservation by exchanging high resource value land for less sensitive lands.

State statutes dealing with urban trust land management also need to be completely revised. The Urban Lands Act has not been seriously revisited since 1981, though it has been amended a number of times. The Arizona Preserve Initiative statute was passed as a separate stand-alone planning process which had no relationship to the Urban Lands Act. The two acts should be restructured into one single planning, development, and disposition process for state land, with a single comprehensive management mandate to realize the greatest possible revenue for the trust while also demonstrating innovative sustainable development practices for the benefit of the entire state.

Finally, revenues from state trust land should be dedicated to education as a cushion on top of other funding, instead of simply replacing dollars from the general fund. Assets purchased, programs funded, and benefits should be specifically highlighted so Arizonans can see what they are getting from trust revenues.

In the Spanish villages of the Southwest, there was a tradition of land held by the community, the *ejido*. It was available to all members of the village for use. The Anglo-American tradition of land ownership was not able to cope with the concept, and as settlement patterns shifted, the ejido was lost to parcelization and development. In most cases, it simply disintegrated a little at a time until none was left, and the community realized no benefit from its passage. State trust land is modern-day Arizona's ejido. We must come to terms with its management, disposition, and development before a unique opportunity is lost.

Getting Around ━━━━━━━━━━━━━━━━━━━━━━━━━━━

Despite repeated costly campaigns proposing mass transit as the solution to traffic congestion and air pollution, metropolitan Phoenix voters have remained extremely skeptical, with considerable justification. Today, the area has the lowest average miles of bus service per capita of all major metropolitan areas in the United States—and spends the least on transit. But the cities touted as "competition" or "success stories" in the transit world highlight the very high costs involved relative to benefits: Portland spends around $250 million a year on its transit systems, capturing 2.5 percent of urban travel. Houston spends nearly $300 million for 2 percent; San Diego, a little under $200 million for 1.5 percent. Proponents of transit point out that these statistics are for total daily trips and that at rush hour the rates are higher but, nevertheless, transit remains an extremely expensive proposition that has not captured the imagination of Phoenicians.

Transit's benefits relative to air pollution are even harder to justify. Even the most ardent advocates of major transit investment are forced to concede that most research indicates that transit is the single most expensive way to reduce levels of unhealthy air. Alternative fuel and auto technologies hold far more promise for lessening air pollution.[1]

In the midst of transportation rhetoric, it is important to recognize some realities. First, the existing development pattern in metropolitan Phoenix essentially requires that every household have an automobile. Nationally, even among households with incomes less than $10,000, more than 60 percent own at least one car or truck,[2] and the rate is even higher in Phoenix. At 1.6 cars per household, our average is among the highest in the world.[3] The need for individual personal mobility vehicles will not change: it is virtually impossible to go shopping, to drop kids off, to exist in Phoenix without a car. Since nearly every household has a car, a fair analysis of transportation costs cannot simply compare the variable costs of driving a car to the variable costs of riding transit. The largest cost of an automobile trip is the capital investment in the automobile. Once that capital investment has been made, an individual consumer's choice is between taking the car or riding transit. The incremental cost of using the car is less and the convenience is much higher. This means that rationally behaving consumers living in an environment in which they must have personal vehicles to survive will continue to favor those personal vehicles over public transit.

Second, it is a common tendency to associate increased traffic with new development. But the change in lifestyle to one of increasing mobility has substantially contributed to increasing traffic. If the baby boomers drove the same amount as their parents had, traffic would have increased by 25 percent between those generations. Instead, between 1969 and 1983, it increased by 56 percent.[4] Even in areas where population is on the decline, traffic often increases. Part of the reason is the change in working and living patterns. We dart out to dinner several times a week, and when we do stay home, we need to go shopping for that night's food. Between 1969 and 1983, per capita miles driven increased by 17 percent. Think about your own driving patterns. Besides a daily commute, how many times a day does your car come and go—to drop off kids, to stop for dinner, to satisfy an impulse at Dairy Queen?

Metropolitan Phoenix residents rank quite high among world cities in the number of daily vehicle miles traveled (DVMT): 21.5 miles in 1994.[5] But this number is significantly lower than Atlanta (34), Dallas (30), and Houston (26). Phoenix is comparable to Minneapolis and Portland. Where Phoenix stands out is in the percentage of travel served by surface streets. In 1994, that figure was 77 percent, the highest of any major metropolitan area in the country. Our ubiquitous grid made up for our lack of freeways. The grid makes our average trips shorter, and often slower.

While everyone in the United States is driving more, Phoenicians don't appear to be out of the ordinary. Because we have always been drivers, our DVMT only went up about ten percent from 1982–92, a smaller increase than in many other areas. During that same period, we dropped from fourth most congested urban area to twenty-first—because of aggressive freeway construction.[6]

Despite all of our grumbling, and despite local press opinions on our rush hour volume, the reality is that the Phoenix metropolitan area has less congestion than most comparable metropolitan areas. The reason is the abundance of routes provided by the grid combined with the dispersal of commuting patterns.

In the 1970s, it was widely believed that mass transit offered real solutions to congestion. But mass transit often has not lived up to its promise because of a dispersal in both trip origins and destinations. For transit to work well, large numbers of trips need to be fed to a single location—like a downtown. In a multicentered place like Phoenix, the commuting patterns are a virtual scramble, with neither end of a majority of trips being fixed.

The failure of sweeping and ambitious programs intended to remake transit in the eyes of the voters was not simply a failure of campaign tactics: the electorate is realistic and sophisticated on this issue. Commuters are rational beings making reasonable economic decisions. Transportation is largely about time. If you can commute in less time in your automobile, you will certainly do so. Even if the time to use your car is only slightly more than riding transit, you will likely use your automobile because it is more convenient, more comfortable, and you may save time later if you need to make a subsequent trip. It is only when there is a significant economic disincentive to auto use, either in time or in cost (e.g., parking), that you will choose an alternate. That disincentive exists in cities like New York, and the policies of San Francisco, Portland, and Seattle that discourage or even prohibit downtown parking are efforts to create the same disincentive.

In the low-density fabric of Phoenix, which was built around the use of the automobile, it is nearly impossible to create disincentives to auto use. There are no new-construction parking requirements in downtown Phoenix, but in the rest of the Valley zoning regulations demand that very high ratios of parking be provided. Even in the downtown, parking is built with every project, because to do otherwise would result in a severe market penalty: no tenants. If we followed the lead of other cities and prohibited more new parking in downtown, the likely result would be no new development downtown.

Outside of downtown, inadequate parking is viewed as a symptom of congestion—not as a cure. A retail center with a 24-screen movie complex was so crowded with cars it convinced the City of Phoenix to reexamine its commercial parking ratios. Large sport utility vehicles are resulting in the repeal of compact-car spaces. Peculiarly in the City of Phoenix, we are so paranoid about parking that the larger an office building gets, the higher the ratio of spaces required—a reverse economy of scale, which is the opposite of the standard used in almost any other city.

The relationship between transportation and land use continues to be a source of controversy. Some citizens, usually when opposing a rezoning near their neighborhood, argue that decreasing density will decrease traffic congestion. Decreasing density does mean fewer people living in a specific area. However, if those people still reside in the area, lowering the density at which they live will increase overall traffic congestion, since each resident will make longer trips. On the other hand, advocates of increased density see living at higher densities as a panacea for transportation problems because when densities are high enough, they believe mass transportation will become viable. The reality is that we cannot retrofit most of the Valley to high enough densities to achieve this vision without bulldozing most of the existing city, nor are most current residents willing to support such high densities anywhere near them. Even under a successful program to actively increase the density of new development, the likely outcome would be a compromise on "medium density" of approximately ten dwelling units per acre. The result? Somewhat more people living in a given area with nearly all of them still driving automobiles, resulting, most probably, in worse congestion.

There is a perception that much of Phoenix's congestion problem resulted because unexpected growth occurred in areas where the transportation infrastructure was inadequate. In fact, in Phoenix, virtually all growth has taken place in areas where it was predicted and planned. The transportation infrastructure is inadequate not because the growth was not anticipated but because we do not build infrastructure in advance of growth. Since we expect growth to "pay for itself," infrastructure is not installed until development takes place, and gaps in timing often result.

We should stop trying to sell Phoenix voters on grandiose visions of transit. Other cities spending more on transit is not sufficient justification to even the score. Because transit works in metropolitan areas with high-density cores does not mean that building a transit system will automatically create dense urbanization here. Rather, we should accept the reality that is Phoenix. This means, first, embracing personal mobility vehicles as the dominant transport mechanism into the future, but figuring out how to better manage their use. Second, there is an appropriate role for realistically and responsively built mass transit.

Cars brought us to this point and continue to structure our lives. We do not want to give that up and it would be nearly impossible to structure this city to function without them. We cannot, and should not, try to change that pattern. Instead, we should think about how to improve transportation efficiency and operation in a personal mobility vehicle–based future. This means we should be at the forefront of transportation innovations focusing on cleaner fuels, alternative vehicle types, pricing mechanisms, and land use patterns that encourage smaller, more efficient cars.

For example, we should logically structure pricing mechanisms with regard to transportation. ADOT's efforts to encourage freeway or express lane user fees has not become reality, but pricing mechanisms are clearly the best way to get at rational transportation decisions. Much of the problem has been an unwillingness to face the political firestorm of charging for roadways that have been free. But tolls are both rational and effective, especially if they are higher at congested periods. Since we are forced to build roads to meet peak demands, peak hour users should pay more.

There are currently areas in which we operate irrational pricing mechanisms, such as exacting a time penalty on those who live closer to their work. When they go to get on the freeway, their access ramp is metered, causing them to be delayed while commuters who live farther out speed past, the reverse of the logical priority. One proposal is simply to toll every on-ramp of the Maricopa Freeway through the Broadway Curve in the morning. The farther south the on-ramp, the higher the toll. The solution is simplistic but real—that is how pricing mechanisms operate. Our metropolitan area is a logical place for widespread experimentation with congestion pricing through electronic sensors and smart cards. Southern California has been led to these alternatives by near catastrophic congestion. We could get there first.

The simplest pricing mechanism is to increase the gasoline tax. We have not indexed the gas tax to rise and fall with the price of gasoline, and a higher tax has the benefit of encouraging more efficient vehicles and more careful use. In an effort to reach some kind of equilibrium with road users paying their fair share of the real costs, gasoline taxes should rise drastically, with some portion of the revenue to be used for buses. The tax does have regressive tendencies, but so does general sales tax, which is how we funded freeways and transit in the past.

Since we already inspect vehicles for excessive polluting, we could add pollution-dependent pricing mechanisms to our license fees, raising revenue and reducing trips by heavily polluting vehicles. Recognizing the continuing efficiency of our ubiquitous grid system of streets, we should also encourage the use of electric vehicles for the huge volume of short shopping trips that take place throughout the metropolitan area. Subdivisions might even be planned with dedicated golf cart paths to connect to neighborhood uses including shopping and parks. What works well in Sun City could be expanded into other master-planned community areas. Thanks largely to General Motors, we have been at the country's forefront in efforts to sell larger electric vehicles for commuting. We could further encourage this result by duplicating California's restrictive emission standards. We are already considered part of the southern California market by many manufacturers.

There is a role for mass transit in the future of Phoenix—even an expanded role. A basic transit system (probably beyond what we have now) is needed as a safety net for citizens who are unable to afford, or to use, a car. That system should be built around the work and shopping patterns of such citizens. Expansion beyond that basic system should be demand driven, which mainly means serving heavily patronized commuting routes. Such an expansion ought not be based on elaborate and inordinately expensive notions of building rail lines or monorails. The cost of fixed rail construction is staggering, as Los Angeles has painfully discovered in its now aborted efforts. Once such an investment is made, rail systems are inflexible. Therefore, they work best when transportation patterns are predictable and long established. Rail transit's best use is to feed large numbers of people to a single point along a series of spoke-like corridors. But the city of the future will have, as Phoenix now does, multiple vital centers which may move about from time to time.

What rail transit does well is to save time in traveling through congested areas. Conventional buses fail on this count. Not only are they less pleasant than personal vehicles, they are typically slower, since they are stuck in the same traffic. Ordinary buses load and unload too slowly compared to rail transit, forcing every passenger through a single door and fare box. There are ways to solve these problems, however, by making buses more like light rail, while still saving over the huge investment of new rail systems.

Curitiba, Brazil, is the world leader in experimenting with high-volume efficient bus transportation. Their systems separate buses onto dedicated traffic lanes in the center of broad boulevards. Traffic signals are wired to give priority to buses as they approach. Passenger loading and unloading occurs through multiple doors from raised platforms, and the fares are collected on the platforms, so the buses can load and unload at the speed of transit vehicles. The system has been built slowly, over 25 years, based on cheap and available technology. The cost is about $2.5 million per mile, compared with the tens or hundreds of millions per mile for a rail system using new or separate rights-of-way.[7]

Metropolitan Phoenix could implement such a system along a street like Washington Street, to connect the state capitol, downtown, the airport, and the university. For a fraction of the cost of a rail system, such a bus route would provide the necessary experiment to see if speedy and efficient mass transit can gain market acceptance. The system could also be easily adapted to the freeway diamond lanes during rush hour. Most importantly, a system based on buses would allow routes to be changed and adapted.

We stand today on the verge of a revolution in the way people live and work every bit as profound as the revolution brought to us by the automobile. The future is a world we cannot fully visualize, much less anticipate. This is not the time to invest large amounts of capital in inflexible transportation systems geared either to the current urban development patterns or, even more fatally, to some nostalgic view of livable cities from a different era.

The digital revolution will permit a much greater range of travel time options—rush hour will begin to wither as more work-related activity becomes increasingly asynchronous. This is a highly desirable phenomenon, since it means less public investment in extremely costly infrastructure (either roads or rail) that is fully utilized only at peak-hour travel times. By encouraging asynchronous work patterns, and making public investments to facilitate such patterns, society can anticipate the future and save public investment. Phoenix is fortunate in being at the forefront of the "wiring" of America. Since such wiring is an investment in public infrastructure which, for the most part, the public does not have to pay for, we should make public rights-of-way easily available for cellular, cable, and phone connections, and we should create incentives for employers to facilitate telecommuting. If we invest public time and energy in understanding and encouraging telecommuting, it will pay a greater dividend than if we continue dreaming about a radical change in transit patterns.

The synchronous activity nodes of the future will be those dealing with pleasure and enjoyment—places where we want to see and interact with one another. These include restaurants and sports and entertainment venues. This coming revolution suggests that the village cores of Phoenix should be repositioned to emphasize entertainment, eating, and face-to-face business meetings, which can take place in hotels or conference centers and certain kinds of specialty shopping areas. These trends are already visible in the success of turning the downtowns of Phoenix and Tempe into entertainment destinations.[8] As work disperses and desynchronizes, social interaction will increase in importance. Urban cores will not disappear, but people's transportation routines will be spread differently—throughout the day and into the evening instead of at peak hours, and they will be geared to special events. Transit has a role in facilitating these uses, related to special sporting events and other mass congregations. But that role is better served by flexible vans, buses, and special-event alternatives than by the heavy investment in a commuting-oriented system.

We ought to recognize this trend in our land use policies. This means that rather than continue to encourage the congregation of major employment uses in village cores, hoping we can figure out a way to handle the transportation needs, we should encourage planned dispersion of employment to perimeter business park locations sited to reduce traffic congestion. High public-contact office uses with retail character, such as travel agencies and brokerage houses and some major employers, will continue to locate in cores, which is appropriate. But incentives for major employment should not be tied to clustering in a limited area. We should instead view cores more as retail and entertainment destinations, designed to spread travel throughout the day.

Throughout the history of the Valley of the Sun there have been times when the civic leadership has felt that the transportation system was lagging behind the area's growth. The railroad came very late. This was the last major metropolitan area to build a serious freeway network. We have the most limited mass transit system of any big city in America. Rather than getting ahead of the curve, the history of transportation in metropolitan Phoenix has been to wait, react incrementally, and build only that which is necessary to keep the area functioning while allowing individual citizens the greatest degree of personal mobility. This unexpressed philosophy of minimum action has actually served the area fairly well. Standing now on the edge of the electronic future, our best bet is to continue that tradition.

Paying for Growth ━━━━━

"All growth should pay for itself." The phrase is a mantra, recited by city councilmembers in speeches, repeated by city managers being interviewed, chanted by planners at conferences—an unquestionable tenet of modern municipal governance. And yet, while this proposition is accepted as an article of faith, these same politicians and bureaucrats pass financial deals to encourage new development, industry, or retail uses with ever more creative incentive packages. Is there any logic operating here?

The question of whether new urban growth pays for itself or occurs at the expense of existing city residents purports to have been exhaustively examined in urban planning and economic development literature. Many of these studies compare, for example, the costs and benefits of different types of urban growth, and generally reach a conclusion that "sprawl" is a more expensive form of urban development than more compact or "better planned" development.[1] Other commentators have extensively reviewed the literature and reached different results.[2]

The problems inherent in these comparative analyses of the costs of development are enormous. One of the problems is how costs are defined, which too often focuses only on the initial public investment in infrastructure to serve a new area. Urban economist Thomas Black has argued that the traditional analysis of development costs fails to take a big enough view, because it should recognize the economic advantages of decreased rent in newer lower-density areas, which is translated into lower business costs and economic benefit. Further, if employment and housing are both dispersed, decreased public investment is needed to construct the mass transit systems necessary to serve high-density cores.[3]

Another problem with cost of growth studies is that they generally represent static snapshots of costs, benefits, cross subsidies, and wealth transfer. A recent study of property taxes and capital expenditures in the City of Phoenix provides an excellent illustration of this point.[4] This study divides the city into three zones: pre-1960, 1960–79, and 1980–90. Based upon an analysis of property taxes only within these zones, it concludes that the "inner" areas are paying proportionately higher property taxes while receiving lower city capital expenditures. The conclusion is likely accurate, but represents a pattern that repeats itself over and over in a growing area: citizens who live in the Arcadia neighborhood near 40th Street and Camelback Road are taxed to pay for new development north of the CAP Canal. Once upon a time, residents of the Palmcroft neighborhood near McDowell Road and 7th Avenue were taxed so the city could install the infrastructure now serving Arcadia.

The balkanizing methodology of isolating a neighborhood within a city to measure the economic revenue/cost sustainability of that precise area is neither realistic nor desirable, and is ultimately meaningless given the vagaries of defining a neighborhood. But more fundamentally, the method itself is flawed: different subsidies flow in different directions at different times. Suburban fringe dwellers may have their new traffic lights subsidized by those who live in an area which already has enough signals; those same fringe dwellers are in turn paying taxes dedicated to building downtown cultural institutions they seldom visit.

Any analysis of this sort is complicated by the different mechanisms which cities use to "charge" for public costs. Property taxes, sales taxes, and impact fees are the chief components. Different mechanisms are often used by overlapping jurisdictions. Arizona schools, for example, have relied upon funding almost entirely from property taxes unrelated to a local municipality. Each charging mechanism has certain characteristic differences of timing, equity, and magnitude. An examination of one revenue variable, while interesting, does not explain the full economic dynamics of growth. Most studies tend to focus on only one variable when examining where a subsidy flows—toward or away from growth—while examining another cost variable might result in the opposite conclusion.

A final problem with the cost-of-growth debate is that most of the dialogue does not even deal with the global issue of whether growth itself is economically good or bad for a region. Instead of analyzing the question of whether or not absolute growth in jobs, population, and economic activity is good or bad or how those factors are related, most planning literature focuses on the physical shape of growth—more specifically, on the economic detriment or benefit of "sprawl." The definition of sprawl is itself highly subjective. In one review of the literature, sprawl is defined as subdivisions and strip commercial developments with large amounts of skipped-over vacant land, residential densities of one-third acre lots or larger, and commercial development with floor area ratios below .20. Planned development, by contrast, has a range of higher residential densities (five or more to the acre) clustered around commercial uses with open space incorporated into the planning areas.[5] By these terms, the development pattern of metro Phoenix, with four to five residential units to the acre, usually in large scale master-planned subdivisions with designated commercial locations clustered at section line corners, is a nearly perfect fit for the "planned development" (non-sprawl) alternative.

Most of the articles on the costs of growth do little beyond validating the preconceived bias of the author. It does seem possible, however, to draw a few simple conclusions about the costs of growth:

1. Very few cities and no major metropolitan area have concluded that it is economically preferable to stop population growth. This conclusion is a recognition that despite all of the studies concluding that there are costs

attendant to growth, if those costs were not ultimately paid by new development, then a growing city would fall farther and farther into deficit. Places like Phoenix and Las Vegas would bankrupt.

2. A relatively large body of literature is devoted to reaching an obvious conclusion: the cost of most public infrastructure necessary to serve urban development is lower on a per capita basis if the development is of a higher density.

3. In those cities where sprawl development is seen as a threat to the existing urban fabric, there are significant negative costs attached to the decline of older central city areas. These costs include increased crime, excess infrastructure capacity from abandonment of older areas, and the need for public investment in redevelopment.[6]

4. There is an inevitable gap between when new development occurs and when it pays for itself. If an area is to continue growing, this gap must be financed through some combination of public and private investment.

The timing of growth costs is critical to thinking about managing the future of a growing community like metropolitan Phoenix. Ultimately, growth has been the basis for the city's financial health. Growth continues to be accepted as economically beneficial. But the short-term consequences of growth can be negative for existing and new residents. Their complaints are most often stated in terms of rate: we are growing too fast—the public infrastructure of roads, utilities, police, schools, and libraries is not keeping up with population.

As a new area is built, single-family homes lead the way. Streets and utilities must be installed in advance of any homes being built, and when homes themselves are built they are sold over a period lasting several years. Residents do not immediately begin paying property taxes, but from the day they move in, they make demands on public infrastructure: they use the streets, their children go to the schools, they insist on vigorous police protection. This new area often does not have any commercial or employment uses. Until there is enough population, a supermarket will not be built. The residents, therefore, drive back to the already developed part of the city to do their shopping. Their sales tax revenue shows up in the form of revenue from existing development rather than new development. While it is being generated by the citizens of the new area, that area will appear to have a deficit in terms of tax receipts. Eventually, when the new area is fully built, it will resemble the established parts of the community, which are economically sustainable in terms of a mix of uses, tax revenues, and demands on infrastructure.

Many advocates of development paying for itself see development impact fees as the solution to this "gap" problem. A development impact fee is levied on every building permit to pay for the incremental additional infrastructure necessary to serve the new area. Prior to impact fees, a city would simply require a developer to dedicate all of the public rights-of-way necessary and build the roads. If major infrastructure, such as water or sewer lines, needed to be extended, that was also typically done by the developer. Sometimes a city, engaging in intelligent forward planning, wanted a developer to install a bigger water or sewer line or a wider street than would be necessary to serve just their own development. In such a case, the city would require the developer to install larger infrastructure, but would work out an arrangement whereby either the city or subsequent developers would reimburse the first developer for the cost of "oversizing."

One of the most critical infrastructure gap problems in Phoenix in the late 1990s was the inadequate road connection between the Ahwatukee-area Mountain Park Ranch and Foothills developments and Interstate 10. Thousands of homes were built with freeway access via a severely sub-standard two-lane Chandler Boulevard. Every day the road jammed up, and residents were furious. The property adjacent to Chandler Boulevard, the developers of which would be required to widen the road, did not develop at the same time. Until that development occurs, it is the policy of the city not to do the needed street widening. Why? Because we believe that development should pay for itself.

Impact fees replace the older system of exactions from adjacent properties with a financial charge on each new dwelling unit or square foot of commercial space. Both the U.S. Supreme Court and Arizona statutes and case law restrict the impact fee amount to be fairly proportional to the infrastructure demands created by the new development. Because of this requirement and the fact that dollars are more easily split up and allocated among multiple parties than actual construction of building improvements could be, impact fees are a theoretically more fair mechanism of spreading the cost of development among new residents. As a result, most cities are moving toward impact fees.

Impact fees, however, do not fully solve the gap problem: an impact fee cannot be assessed until something is actually built, but the first thing that must be built is the public infrastructure, which is supposed to be paid for by the impact fees—a chicken or the egg dilemma. The use of impact fees to fund growth is in conflict with the concept of concurrency—that development should not take place unless and until there is adequate infrastructure in place to serve the development. Yet many politicians purport to believe in both, failing to see the conflict.

Impact fees are complex, and require elaborate implementation to ensure they are fair.[7] One complexity is how to fairly apportion costs of development between different kinds of land uses. North of the CAP Canal, Phoenix assesses impact fees based on "equivalent dwelling units" (EDUs: a house is one EDU). For street construction, the EDU system assigns the cost of streets based on how many trips per day are generated by different land uses. A single-family home generates ten trips per day, a convenience market or a fast food restaurant may generate a thousand trips per day. The conclusion of this methodology, therefore, is that the fast food restaurant should pay an impact fee 100 times as great as the single-family home.

There may be all sorts of reasons why we do not like fast food restaurants. But if there is not a Burger King built near new homes, the residents will probably drive to another fast food restaurant farther away. Some of them may decide to stay home, but many of them will simply drive a greater distance to patronize a Burger King built somewhere else. Eliminating the restaurant does not eliminate the trips. It does mean that the people in the houses will actually drive farther on the street network than if fast food was nearby. The overall result of eliminating the restaurant is to put a greater burden on public infrastructure. In the City of Phoenix, full impact fees are charged only north of the CAP canal, a recognition of the huge investment in infrastructure that was needed to open that area to development. The result of the commercial impact fee assessment mechanism, however, has been to discourage commercial development, causing residents in that area to drive greater distances south into already developed areas or into Scottsdale, where the fees are lower.

One of the most serious and systemic gap problems is in regard to schools. Education finance in Arizona is a mess, and currently has two major crisis points. The first is the inequality between rich and poor districts, which has forced the courts to repeatedly find the state's education finance system unconstitutional. The second is the inability of fast-growing districts to build schools quickly enough to match population growth. Solutions to the problem of inequity may actually exacerbate the fast-growth gap because they need to eliminate local bonding authority. This disadvantages new areas with high tax bases. Fairly structured, education impact fees could provide a solution, if property taxes were adjusted in the impact fee area to eliminate double charging.[8]

Paying for growth is a complicated issue not well suited to shallow analysis, cute slogans, or political posturing. The statement that growth should pay for itself means little if divorced from the question of how soon the new development should become self-sustaining. The cost of municipal governance is the cost of structuring life in an orderly society, the price we pay as parties to the social compact. Each of us at some point probably is paying more than our fair share, and at some other point is being subsidized. The trick is in achieving long-term equity and stability.

Classic conservative dogma holds that government should not provide special tax breaks or other incentives to encourage business. Such incentives can distort the efficiency of the market or create a market that should not exist. Once enacted, incentives become hard to abolish, since they create constituencies. Yet, pro-business elected officials, who generally think of themselves as conservatives, are often willing to create incentives in support of economic activity. This is especially the case with city councilmembers, who see their city as a business in competition with other cities to attract and retain jobs and companies, and who, therefore, are willing to use government incentives to increase their city's competitiveness.

In conservative Arizona, the conflict between these two principles—avoiding government interference in the marketplace or using government to support economic development—have led to an often irrational Rube Goldberg system of economic incentives employed by local governments as enticements for businesses to enter a community. The system is not predictable, policy based, or consistent—all of which ought to be basic requirements of any government intervention in market activity.

One of the earliest uses of city-sponsored incentives began as a redevelopment mechanism. Arizona had enacted standard municipal redevelopment statutes in the 1950s allowing municipalities to assemble land through condemnation and resell it for redevelopment. The city might resell the land below its actual assemblage cost, but with the requirement that the buyer commit to build new development beneficial to the area. In many states, cities can also give such a developer a break in property taxes, using either tax abatement (eliminating the property taxes for some period of time) or tax increment financing (freezing the taxes at the level prior to the new development). The Arizona legislature has steadfastly refused to explicitly authorize these techniques in Arizona, largely because of the opposition of conservative business groups and local school districts, which would lose revenue.

Creative bureaucrats and developers realized that once the city had acquired title to a redevelopment site, it could lease the property to the developer instead of selling it, and thus hold title to the land and the new buildings. As city-owned property, the development would not be put on the county tax rolls, creating de facto tax abatement. Several Arizona cities began structuring such deals, negotiating with each redeveloper how long the abatement period would be, after which ownership would shift back into private hands.

In 1985 the legislature, concerned with this procedure, enacted a statute taxing the leasehold interest in municipal property as if the property were titled in private hands.[9] The statute allowed certain exceptions, including a right to continue using the mechanism for tax abatement in downtown redevelopment areas, but only for eight years. Cities stretched their definitions of downtown so broadly that a number of private developers protested the continued use of tax abatement as unfair competition. In 1996, after the courts also found aspects of the new tax unconstitutional, the legislature again revisited the issue, creating a new Government Property Lease Excise Tax.[10] This tax is based on square footage rather than value (in order to avoid constitutional problems), and is applied to the property titled to a city but leased to a private developer. The tax continues to allow exemptions for limited periods in redevelopment areas.

Incentives can be useful, and sometimes they are necessary to spur redevelopment. To assemble and redevelop land carries with it a substantial cost premium compared to the development of raw land. A city faced with a declining area in which it has a substantial investment of physical and social infrastructure needs tools to make redevelopment more attractive and economical. The problem with the existing scheme in Arizona is that, because of the reluctance of the legislature to simply recognize this need and create a straightforward incentive process, cities and private developers have had to patch together a crazy quilt of complicated, and at times risky, mechanisms. The entire tax abatement structure is based on the city holding title to what is not actually a public building. Only sophisticated development companies doing large projects can use these incentives, because only such projects can afford the substantial legal costs of documenting the complicated deals and can satisfy lenders' requirements to ensure that the risk in surrendering title is acceptable. What we have created is a difficult-to-use incentive for big, well-financed projects.

Over the years, bits and pieces of other tax relief incentives have been cobbled onto university property, foreign trade zone sites, and an ever-expanding definition of what is an amusement park. Most of these have been created by statutes enacted in response to a specific lobbying effort, with little attention to programmatic goals. Obtaining these benefits for a major employer or development has little to do with the quantity or quality of future jobs, or whether the use fits into a plan for economic activity we want to encourage. The incentives, as structured, turn instead on quirks of location and the sophistication of a company's ability to work the system. To their credit, a number of cities—notably Tempe—have expressly conditioned their participation in incentives on reviewing issues including average wages, percentage of employees likely to live in the city, and the multiplier effect on the local economy of dollars spent by a company. But this kind of analysis is not consistent from one city to the next, and in some cities is absent altogether.

In today's highly mobile environment, where high-tech and information-based businesses can be located nearly anywhere in the world, major companies stage competitions in which local jurisdictions, and sometimes states themselves, compete with one another in structuring subsidies to lure new businesses. Arizona has often found itself at a disadvantage in such competitions because we have no comprehensive system of incentives. For a long time we believed that sunshine and cheap houses would be incentive enough.

But as we began losing out in competitions, we started using various methods to scrape together packages. Doing so under our illogical system continues to have major disadvantages—often incentives can be offered only at one or two locations, which may not be suitable for the user. The only alternative has been to create a one-time deal and seek legislative approval, a cumbersome and slow process, which itself creates disadvantages.[11]

In metropolitan Phoenix, the most common incentive of all is for a city to create a means of rebating sales taxes generated by a major retail project. In Arizona, local government is inordinately dependent upon sales tax to fund its operations, and it is one of the few aspects of municipal revenue which is easily influenced by local decisions. Our infatuation with sales tax is part of historic pro-growth attitudes and expectations—newcomers, tourists, and future generations will pay the tax.[12]

Walk into a city hall in Maricopa County today and utter the magic words "auto dealer," and city management will begin Pavlovian salivation. Because sales tax is so important, and because major tax generators began demanding to get some of the revenue they generate in tax returned to them, another set of incentives has been created. Most commonly, cities will refund a percentage of sales taxes generated by the development up to a maximum. The dollars will reimburse the developer for certain specified and required public improvements: streets, sewer and water, landscaping.

There is nothing wrong with a city seeking, in an entrepreneurial fashion, to increase its tax base. However, oftentimes coveting a retail use does not represent new economic activity. Rather, one jurisdiction is attempting to prosper to the detriment of its neighbor. Sales tax revenues are enhanced by retail uses, but the jobs created are often low-wage and unstable.

There are several important changes that we should implement with regard to paying for growth. For example, municipal government's obsession with sales tax distorts land use patterns and leads cities to fight one another for their piece of a limited pie. We should either reduce the proportionate reliance or create metropolitan-wide means of sharing some portion of sales taxes. Sales tax incentive rebates should also be rationalized and offered relatively sparingly for uses that are unusually beneficial or serve to implement important land use policies.

Growth costs should become a mandated element of all community general plans. Cities should explain their intended means of covering growth costs and the city's position on competing goals of infrastructure concurrency and making development pay for itself. Each city should have a goal for how quickly new development is expected to cover its costs, and what revenues will be counted in reaching a balance.

Impact fees are one appropriate means of apportioning costs when properly administered, but they are not a panacea. Cities must continue to use a full range of public financing options to install public infrastructure. Individual cities should be able to make development in certain areas easier by using public money to install infrastructure, so long as they reveal and justify such a decision.

We need a comprehensive state framework for the use of incentives. Instead of being unwilling to face the need for such mechanisms in today's business environment, we should clearly spell out the process so that cities and the private sector have an equal understanding and ability to use the appropriate incentives. Those uses eligible for incentives ought to be established as part of a regional economic development plan. Cities could have different criteria—for example, another credit card processing operation may not be needed in Tempe, but might be highly desirable in Peoria. Most important, some effort must be made to establish criteria in advance of a particular proposal. A city should not wait to respond on an ad hoc basis to proposals offered by a new user, and the user should not have to hire a private consultant to lead them through the maze of "let's make a deal" city relationships.

Incentives should be provided directly to desired uses, not to a particular location. The user should choose the best site for their needs, regardless of whether the land is publicly or privately owned, providing a level playing field among developments rather than an unfair advantage for publicly supported real estate entrepreneurship. We should not provide incentives for speculative development, except in genuine downtown redevelopment areas, and then for the limited purpose of turning around an area in decline.

In devising mechanisms to pay for growth, we should not be disguising an effort to discourage growth, or to change its shape, density, or form. If we want to do any of those things, we need to honestly and fairly debate whether we want higher density, less commercial, slower development, or more open space, and reach a conclusion. Paying for growth is about paying for government, and it comes subsequent to planning the shape of our city. Too often we do the opposite—create a financial mechanism that may be palatable to the electorate, and let the shape of development follow. Or we pick a financing system hoping it will slow down growth. Both of those alternatives represent dangerous extremes, not intelligent policies.

And the Process Is the Substance ───────

The city council chamber is a round building, a legacy of the Sputnik era when branch banks were designed to look like flying saucers. Tonight the room is packed with an assortment of angry people wearing red octagonal buttons. There is too much lettering to read the buttons from were the city council sits, but the message is clear: STOP a development proposal. Unfortunately, the case at issue is number 14 on a long agenda. By the time it is called the hour will be close to midnight. Between now and then the council will vote on convenience stores, shopping centers, a slew of subdivisions, and at least two apartment complexes which themselves have a dozen or more opponents in the audience.

Just before the meeting starts, six zoning lawyers in expensive suits mill around joking with one another. Between them they are involved in nearly every case on the agenda, and so they try to estimate what time the hearing will end. There are a few other citizens who know their way around— groupies of the zoning process, perennial neighborhood activists, members of committees which have reviewed some of the developments. They join the lawyers in a betting pool on the length of the hearing, and exchange gossip about how the councilmembers might vote.

At about 11:15 the case that has drawn the red buttons gets underway. The tallest of the lawyers, who has already won two cases earlier on the agenda, explains his request to rezone a vacant 12-acre parcel located at the intersection of two section line roads on the far northern edge of the city. The area is shown on the general plan map as developing at two to five dwelling units to the acre, but three of the four surrounding sides are vacant. To the west are a series of existing residences, all built on one-acre lots. The lawyer explains why his request should be approved: "The planning commission and planning staff support our request. There is an increasing need for commercial services in the area. Cur-rently, residents are driving nearly six miles to get groceries, and the closest store is in another jurisdiction, which is getting their taxes. The general plan indicates that the area surrounding this site will eventually have thousands of homes, and those citizens will need places to shop. By designating this site now, you can be ahead of the curve in indicating were the commercial should go. This site itself is not shown on the general plan, of course, because it is too small. Your policies recognize, however, that section-line corners are appropriate commercial locations.

"Several of the neighboring citizens have been opposed to the case, and as a result of a written protest filed by two of those neighbors the rezoning requires approval by a three-quarters majority of the city council. But the five other adjacent neighbors are here tonight in support with the package of stipulations which we have worked out. Those stipulations limit the height of the commercial buildings, prohibit deliveries after 9:00 at night or before 8:00 in the morning, and require an extraordinary amount of landscape buffering between our project and the homes. As you can see from these elevations, we have designed the center to have a Santa Fe theme, which has been very well received."

When he finishes, the councilmembers ask a few questions. They focus on the stipulations about landscaping and hours of operation. The city staff explain their support for the proposal and voice their agreement that it is desirable to designate the site as a shopping center even though it may not be built for several years. The mayor calls for supporters of the case, and one neighbor stands up.

"I live immediately adjacent to the project. We were initially strongly opposed. We moved out here to be away from congestion and commercial. But we realize that development is coming, we can't stop it. We sat down with the developer and negotiated the stipulations you see. With those protections, we can live with this. We realize that this site is on the corner of two busy roads and is not likely to develop for single-family homes. We'd rather have a well-designed center with stipulations than any form of higher density housing."

Next, the mayor indicates that there are about 60 cards turned in by people wanting to speak in opposition. Five have indicated that they are the spokespersons for the larger group, so he calls on them in order.

"My name is Fred Jacobs. My family and I live about a half mile from the site. We have lived there for eight years, on a two-acre lot with our two children and three horses. We drive to the store once a week, but we don't go to the one six miles over, we go south for eight miles. We like it that way. We don't need more services, we moved here to get away from all that. This center would just bring people, houses, congestion, and traffic. The people out here don't want the services, the commercial. We don't want to look like the rest of town."

"I'm Lillian Bindleman. This site is beautiful desert and they would turn it into a parking lot. I could maybe see a little commercial, like a cute restaurant or even a cowboy bar. But no one should be allowed to bulldoze what's there for another Safeway. We have enough. And another one is already planned four miles east. That will be plenty."

"I'm Sam Lemon and I also live adjacent to the site. When I bought my lot two years ago I was assured by the broker that this site was zoned only for one-acre homes and that there was no plan to change it. This center would devalue my property. I'd have to sit in my backyard and look at the rear end of a grocery store where now I can see the McDowell Mountains. I don't care about extra landscaping, I don't want to see this there at all."

This goes on for another 45 minutes, with the audience applauding each speaker, even after the mayor asks them not to. Then the lawyer offers his rebuttal: "You've just heard from people living as far as five miles from this site. They'd like to have the whole north end of the city develop in one-acre homesites with horse privileges—just like where they live. But it's not going to. The general plan shows this area for a density of two to five units to the acre. That means subdivisions with production housing. Some of those subdivisions have already been approved and more are on their way. The people you've heard from mean well, and they like their particular lifestyle, but the city has grown out to where they live. The area will change regardless of whether you vote for this case. The growth is here; it will overwhelm this area in the next two years. You know it, I know it, and this entire audience knows it.

So what should you do? Plan. That's what your staff is suggesting: figure out where the commercial sites should be and designate them. And clearly this is an appropriate site. I understand the people like Sam who'd rather live adjacent to vacant desert or one-acre lots, but it's not realistic, and we've worked really hard to work out a package of stipulations to protect the neighbors."

At 11:47 the councilman from the district, a chiropractor, health entrepreneur, and part-time new age philosopher who also lives on a one-acre lot moves to deny the case, explaining: "No proposal which generates this much negative energy should be approved. I applaud the efforts of the developer to work this out, but they just haven't done enough. Maybe some of the stores could be eliminated, or fewer parking spaces or a different design, but until more residents are satisfied, I just can't vote yes." His motion to deny is defeated by a three to four vote.

A motion to approve is then offered by a councilmember from another part of the city. She is a realtor by profession, and explains that she agrees with the staff—there's going to be development, so let's do it right. Her motion gets a five to two vote in favor, with one councilmember switching votes from the first motion, but under the "super majority" required because of the written protest, that is not three-quarters of the full council, so the motion fails. The rezoning is denied.[1]

Variations of this scenario are repeated in jurisdictions throughout the Valley on almost any weekday night. Sometimes the controversy is about a parcel in an established area of town where a more intense land use, such as apartments, is planned. Existing residents will likely oppose the project, based on increased traffic and the perception that renters are bad citizens who bring crime with them. Sometimes the proposal is for a large office building, which is threatening because of traffic or because citizens fear it will block their views or invade the privacy of their backyards. If a high-tech plant is planned, pollution and traffic are the problems. And sometimes there will be opposition to even more houses just like the ones already there, because of traffic, crowded schools, and vague anger at the pace of change.

These cases have a series of common threads: we did not know this might happen when we moved here; it is the city council's job to respond to angry voters at a public hearing; the developer should work hard to cut a deal with the neighbors. And so we build our city: a deal at a time, pursuant to an incremental decision at midnight.

In Anglo-American jurisprudence, there are two broad traditions of how we make societal decisions. One is judicial in character. We take a dispute to a wise man, a shaman, a judge, and ask him to rule based on what is right. Judicial decision making is predicated on finding the correct answer to a conflict based on the application of a series of principles drawn from past decisions. It holds consistency to be the highest value. Decisions should not vary depending on personal feelings. We have crafted a vast and elaborate system around this goal: rules of evidence, sworn testimony, limitations on contacting the wise man outside of a formal hearing, due process.

The other decision-making tradition is that of the village elders: legislative. Legislative decision making has as its paramount goal not consistency but responsiveness. The will of the people is at stake. There is no absolute right and wrong; the only principle is usually majority rules. Depending on who has the votes, different decisions are made in similar circumstances, or a decision already made may be changed. A legislator may vote a particular way for any reason, no reason, or because of who last talked to him at a cocktail party.

Usually, the legislative model is used for the big decisions: passing new laws applicable to society as a whole. The judicial model is used to resolve particular disputes between individuals. Both of these systems are used in the world of land use regulation. Passing a comprehensive zoning ordinance is legislative. Approving a variance to allow a structure to encroach on a setback or exceed the maximum amount of lot coverage is quasi-judicial, meaning it is often ruled upon by a hearing officer or board of adjustment which is, to a degree, bound by rules and precedents.

In Arizona, we approve an exceptionally high percentage of our new development through the process of individual rezoning cases. In part, we do this because we have so much new development on land that has not been previously used. It is also easier to wait until there is a proposal on the table, which we can review and bargain over. It means that the process tends to be driven by a property owner's request, consistent with our strong views on private property rights. Ad hoc legislative decision making is also consistent with our state's deep populist traditions.

Unfortunately, a corollary of reliance on the legislative model is to diminish the significance of planning in guiding growth and development. Instead of the community's general plan being the focus of discussion, the most important consideration becomes whether the immediately adjacent neighborhood can be mollified with additional landscaping, elaborate stipulations, personal contact, and negotiations. Sometimes these negotiations result in a better project, sometimes not. But the focus is seldom on the best interests of the community as a whole.

There are advantages to a system in which most development decisions are legislative. It is often quicker and cheaper than the quasi-judicial models used in such places as Washington and Oregon. There, zoning hearings may go on for hours or even days, witnesses are sworn, and it is difficult to participate without a lawyer.[2] In Arizona, an entire zoning case is usually over in about six months, and a hearing seldom lasts more than three hours. But too often our dialogue about development is lost in the minutia of more trees, a different roofline, the location of driveways. The process of decisions becomes the substance. Restructuring the process is often the best way to produce different results, and thereby to begin shaping growth differently.

It is time to completely rethink our development approval process. I reach this conclusion after a lot of reflection and with some personal trepidation. The existing process is wonderfully dependent on well-compensated zoning lawyers, which I have appreciated for the last few decades. However, our current approach to development decisions is too narrow, too particularized, and too ad hoc. It leads to overly contentious hearings; occasional rezoning by surprise; the politicizing of what, in the scheme of managing a city, are very minor decisions; and a let's-make-a-deal focus on the trivia of development. We need to replace this with a system in which land use is driven by the community general plan, in which those uses are fully and plainly disclosed to surrounding property owners, and in which they change only after careful and deliberate consideration.[3]

The recently enacted Growing Smarter Act[4] makes definite progress in this regard. In response to the threatened urban growth boundary initiative, Governor Hull and the legislature crafted this legislation as an alternative. Most publicized was the provision, now passed into law by the voters, that would dedicate a revenue stream for open space acquisition. But, in addition, a series of changes in the planning enabling acts were enacted into law. These include mandating additional general plan elements dealing with urban form, open space, and growth. The growth element requires large cities to identify future growth areas and conservation areas. To adopt or amend general plans, additional public dissemination is required. General plans and major amendments must be approved by a two-thirds majority vote of the city council.[5]

Growing Smarter also changes the relationship between general plans and zoning by explicitly requiring that zoning and rezoning "conform" to the general plan. Previously, the Arizona standard has been a looser "be consistent with" standard, which has been interpreted by case law to be quite vague. Any future rezoning that does not conform with the general plan—defined as land uses, densities, or intensities of use beyond the range identified by the general plan—would require a general plan amendment, tripping the two-thirds majority vote requirement.

These recent changes are good, but too timid. The general plan must be the driving factor in a community's development. Land uses conforming to the plan ought to be approved with little or no debate about the use itself, moving directly to a review of the site plan and design. This should be true even of a land use requiring a rezoning—if it conforms to the general plan it should not be the subject of long debate, contentious council hearings, super majority requirements at the council level, or of voter referendum.

The simple way to look at the relationship between the general plan and rezoning is to return to the legislative/judicial decision-making models. General plans must become the land use policy-driving regulation. Those plans need to be sufficiently definitive and specific to give reasonable notice to citizens of what sort of development is to occur. General plans and their amendment should be regarded as the stuff of legislation, subject even to referendum to the voters. Rezoning, on the other hand, ought to be regarded as the implementation of the legislative policy expressed in the general plan.[6] The existing statutes providing that the protest by a handful (or in some cases only one) neighbor invokes a three-quarters city council vote ought to be repealed. These statutes distort the focus from the community and its plan to whether the adjacent neighbors have been mollified by stipulations and promises.

Individual rezonings conforming to general plans need to become administrative (or quasi-judicial) in character—the province of hearing officers, not of city councils. Such decisions need not even be appealable to a city council, and certainly should not be the subject of a referendum. Currently any rezoning decision is subject to referendum petitions being circulated, resulting in the case being put on a citywide ballot. The number of signatures required is miniscule—8,000 in the City of Phoenix, less than 2,000 in Scottsdale, Tempe, or Glendale. Because we allow such petitions to be circulated by professionals being paid by the signature, the mechanism is easily abused by anyone wanting to stop a development project—a disgruntled group wanting private land to remain undeveloped, or even a competing landowner wanting to protect personal business interests. An individual project can often be killed simply by the circulating petitions, because if the matter is put on the ballot it may delayed two years.

Planning individual land uses by plebiscite is foolish and bad government. Reducing issues of growth management to slogans and project-by-project up-or-down votes results in paralysis, not intelligent growth management. Public votes are appropriate only on the broadest, truly legislative, policy decisions—the community general plan. Even then, the numbers required to qualify a measure for the ballot should be greatly increased.[7]

Making the process less political is only part of the solution. The system also needs to be better understood. The current combination of the average citizen's lack of knowledge as to how development approval works, coupled with frequent misrepresentation of what is likely to built on a vacant parcel is a recipe for frustration, anger, and alienation. While it is impossible to idiot-proof anything, we can at least require that in every residential home sales transaction there be an explicit disclosure of the city general plan and existing zoning for the area surrounding the home being sold, and a disclosure statement explaining how zoning or the general plan can be changed. The buyer should be required to read and sign off on the disclosure statement.

We need to teach about local government and the planning and development process in our high school civics classes. This is the front line of the social compact: the part of government the average person is most likely to encounter. We teach about the separation of powers at the federal level, but explain virtually nothing about government's power to regulate the use of private property. Our system of land—privately owned but government regulated—is one of the most fundamental tenets of American democracy. But based on the crowds at zoning hearings, the average citizen believes either that "the government" gets to decide exactly what is built, or, at the opposite extreme, that we are entitled to do whatever we want with our property.

A well-informed citizenry and a less political plan-driven approval process would go a long way in making the future Valley of the Sun a better place to live. A vision of a more predictable process may not seem very graphic or inspiring. But cities in a capitalist democracy are ultimately shaped more by process than by design, and so designing the process may be more fruitful than designing the city.

Conclusion

The walk up is short and steep, starting on the west side and climbing the south face toward the stadium. From close up, the butte is rockier and more natural than it looked from the air—clearly not the result of a bulldozer. Sections of it do show the scars of human activity. Two huge water tanks are not really disguised by the palo verdes planted in front of them. Just below the tanks is the yellow letter A, covered with dozens of layers of fraternity-applied paint. The stadium itself took out an entire side of the little mountain, and skyboxes built like bunkers on stilts pop up nearly even with the summit. The last 50 feet of the path are concrete stairs of irregular height and climbing them is an intensely aerobic experience. The stairs end at a locked gate that protects the radio towers on top from the public.

There are people living in Tempe who have climbed the butte every day for 30 years. But until today I probably hadn't climbed it in 30 years. The trail is more civilized than it used to be, with asphalt paving at least halfway up. I doubt it is easy to find pottery shards anymore on the north side, near the riverbed. And I won't try scrambling on the rocky part below the top where I got stuck for two hours when I was fourteen. The biggest difference of all is in the look of the air over the city—browner and more tangible than I remembered.

All the ingredients of desert urbanism are visible from here: the dry bed of the Salt River, impounded and controlled 60 miles northeast; the airplanes lining up to land at Sky Harbor; the freeway headed toward downtown Phoenix; the suburban spread of the East Valley. A few miles east is metropolitan ground zero—Pueblo Grande, the most approachable remnant of the Hohokam.

Transformation is palpable. Construction cranes dot the view in every direction. Just below, Mill Avenue and ASU together form one of the "vital centers" of the region, where people choose to congregate, mixing work and play. Other such nodes of concentration are visible in downtown Phoenix and north toward Scottsdale. At the bottom of the butte's south side, Tempe is considering a mass transit station. On the north side of the river, low- and mid-rise offices are being built close to the airport and to the freeway. A year from now there will be water in the riverbed. An inflatable dam will back up Tempe's Town Lake, impounding 2,500 acre-feet of water, pumped 200 miles from the Colorado River and put back in the bed of a river we dried up to make this city work. When friends and relatives come from out of town, that's where we'll take them, to look at the water.

Vision is a tricky thing, even for individuals. Minds as brilliant as Soleri's and Wright's offered widely differing views of how society should structure settlement. Most of us are not far-sighted enough to concoct similar pictures, nor brave enough to offer a private vision for public critique. Like George Bush, we find the "vision thing" not our cup of tea. Put me in that category.

A consensus vision is even harder to obtain since it requires the simplicity to be understood and shared. Sometimes such a consensus does emerge, but may be unrecognized except by the choices of the marketplace. During the past half century, the Valley of the Sun has not lacked a vision, as is often alleged. We have held a simply stated, powerful, dominating vision: growth. It was an easy, understandable goal we worked toward, and reached. Most children initially have a similarly simple life mission—to get big. Sometime in adolescence the frightening reality of maturity begins to glimmer, and the time comes for more sophisticated yardsticks of success. As our city passes through its adolescence, we are beginning to recognize the same reality, and our previous vision is beginning to unravel. By a margin of more than three to one, citizens of Phoenix believe the city is growing too fast.[1] The clashes over growth are increasingly uncivil. The consensus is lost.

Public opinion polls show strong support for almost any sort of growth control measure. The advocates of such measures often live the very lifestyle they indict, criticizing the past consensus their actions support. If the schools are too crowded, the air too polluted, the parking lots too full, there must be someone to blame. It must be the developers, they've got to be stopped.

The reality of growth is subtle and complex and seldom attributable to scapegoats. The people who complain of anti-social behavior by developers were probably buyers from another fiendish capitalist. They moved because they heard the public schools were good, only to complain because the new arrivals mean the schools are crowded. As absurdly conflicted as these public attitudes can be, they are not altogether wrong. If we do nothing to change, there are very real risks that the negative externalities of existing development patterns will increase to the point of severely impairing the quality of life that is the foundation upon which growth was built. The unchecked free market is not always the best solution, for quality of life itself too easily becomes another tragedy of the commons in which no one is able to recognize and respond to the externality of his own choice, but the aggregate choices of each such individual deteriorate the resource, in this case the lifestyle itself.

Simply discarding the old consensus is not enough. A new vision of our city cannot be only that our old vision was bad. We have to find a new vision of what to be, not what to avoid. Creating that vision will be neither quick nor easy. It will take time, a lot of suggestions (some of them bad), trial and error, and continued debate. There are some steps we can take to help further the evolutionary process.

Step one: Understand why Phoenix is the way it is

Nearly forty years ago Jane Jacobs observed the richly textured street life of Greenwich Village and taught us lessons about human behavior and urban life.[2] Her contribution to understanding American cities is seminal, but too often regarded as an ode to the virtues of high-density living and pedestrian scale. More important was her explanation that cities are the products of millions of tiny decisions about how and where to live, to shop, to eat, to work, and to play. She realized that many of the best urban environments are those that just happen—the result of the ongoing interaction of human beings living together. She attacked what she saw as the then-fashionable school of city planning thought, which called for separation of uses and classes and offered grand modernist visions of monumental city building.

Today we are in jeopardy of losing the real message of Jacobs' insight. Rather than apply the same observational efforts to understanding the new cities of the American West, too many critics want to impose the shape, form, and values of Greenwich Village through a new kind of planning dictate. But impressing a nineteenth-century urban character on places like Phoenix is no more appropriate than was forcing a Bauhaus vision of glass slabs in granite plazas on the dense and variegated urban form of New York. Jacobs' point is as valid as ever: cities are living organisms built chiefly not of conspiracies by shadowy power brokers, but of thousands of incrementally rational decisions by consumers and citizens, influenced and directed—but never controlled—by government actions. Some of those actions are overtly about urban land use, development, growth, and planning. But at least as influential in the West are societal decisions about the importance of agriculture, the portability of water, the value of home ownership, and the need for highway systems.

Phoenix is a result of these factors. Located at a convenient place to collect and redistribute water in an arid environment, the city's roots are agricultural. Water concentrated development within the Salt River Valley, even as heat and the sparse landscape contributed to a thinner dispersion of population than in older cities. The difficulty of surviving in a harsh and forbidding landscape turned early residents into missionary zealots determined to convince others that they should join in building a city and enjoying the benefits of sunshine and dry air.

The city grew slowly until air conditioning and air travel made it possible to virtually ignore an isolated desert location. After the war, those technologies joined with automobiles and a national obsession to provide Americans with single-family homes to create the urban fabric that exists today: a thousand-square-mile oasis of ranch homes, back yards, shopping centers, and dispersed employment based on personal mobility.

146

Step two: Build on the strengths of past growth

The formula for growing worked. Most Phoenicians live in detached single-family homes which they own. The lifestyle of Phoenix still attracts tens of thousands of migrants every year—the marketplace's continuing endorsement of the elements of life here. Despite the angst about growing too fast, the citizens of greater Phoenix continue to express a high degree of satisfaction with the overall quality of life.[3] Objective indicators confirm that in overall comparisons with other metropolitan areas, greater Phoenix fares relatively well.[4]

Our vision should be built on this success, not on a decision that the past growth of metropolitan Phoenix was some colossal mistake. The relentless criticism of detached single-family homes, automobiles, shopping centers, and low-density urban form as "sprawl" does not help us find a new vision. Draconian growth limits, high residential densities, severe financial penalties on new development, and vast mass transit schemes are offered as a fix for our problems. But for Phoenix, that vision collides with existing reality and past history. The vision suggests we re-create what never was: a traditional industrial-age city. If we set out on a deliberate course to make the city denser, we are limited in what we can do by the existing built environment. Unless we intend the wholesale bulldozing of viable neighborhoods, the most we might realistically accomplish is to double or triple our existing density, creating a metropolitan area approximating Los Angeles, the thing we constantly say we are afraid of becoming.

The source of a new vision must not be to deny the force of our history, but to embrace it. Not to radically alter the development patterns that brought the city its boom, but to subtly shift those patterns to preserve the benefits of our lifestyle while mitigating the downsides. Our ranch house subdivisions and shopping centers are not something to be derided, but to be celebrated and rejuvenated. Mass-produced suburban ranch homes are to Phoenix what Victorians are to San Francisco, brownstones to Philadelphia, or bungalows to Los Angeles—a signature of the lifestyle heritage upon which a city is built. This city is a realized vision of the post-war American dream, a city of car-driving, middle-class, consumer homeowners. As Kenneth T. Jackson has recognized, the 1,000-square-foot ranch house directly affected more American lives than all the surviving eighteenth-century mansions together.[5] Our city is the repository of much of this rich heritage. Recognizing the strengths of our urban past is the first step in figuring out how to influence future development.

Step three: Think about how life should be at a point in the future

Cities and counties sometimes use a formal visioning process when they update their comprehensive plans. Such a process calls for citizens to pick an arbitrary point 25 or 50 years hence and try to envision how their city should be. A number of Valley cities and MAG have used this process to try and derive a blueprint, however vague, for guiding future growth.

The concept is a good one if it is grounded in some sense of reality and tied to probable development patterns. In Chapter 7, I suggested using a more radical variation of this technique—trying to project a sustainable population horizon as the point of view. The horizon comes from asking the question: is there a foreseeable limit to growth that should be projected and used for planning? In our case, there is. Water, not land, is the resource that defines this place, and that we ought to respect in creating a horizon. Making choices about water use will determine whether farming survives in any form in central Arizona. If we decide that farming is important, we should take steps to preserve its viability, including using a population horizon that preserves water for agriculture. The result of such an exercise would be to select a future vision of a community of perhaps seven million people in the Phoenix metropolitan area.

It is possible to envision a future city of seven million built in a pattern much like our current metropolis—a community of detached single-family homes at a relatively uniform density of between 2,500 and 3,000 citizens per square mile. If we reach a "population horizon" of seven million in our current development pattern, we will still have urbanized only about half of the land in Maricopa County. This is a likely future, but an acceptable one only if we make a series of changes in the way we currently manage growth and development. A fundamental beginning is to embrace a degree of regional cooperation that we have not previously been willing to entertain. The vision of a city of seven million based on our current values requires that we take steps to save meaningful and accessible desert, preserve personal mobility by dispersing travel patterns, and preserve existing single-family neighborhoods while building new ones that will maintain themselves into the future.

Step four: Create mechanisms today to nudge us toward an acceptable future

Trying to shape the growth of a place like Phoenix is to shoot at a moving target: the whole trick is in anticipating the trajectory and figuring out where to aim. Small adjustments can have major effects. Government's power to shape cities is greatest when exercised in reasonable increments, and we should therefore make carefully measured changes in our regulatory mechanisms. So the next step, then, is to use the power of government to reinforce those trends that lead to a desirable future, while discouraging those which do not.

The desert really is the magic of this place, and we must better understand how to preserve it, and how to live in it. Preservation should be integrated with development, dispersed throughout the region and connected together. Literally billions of dollars should be permanently dedicated to this end.

Next, we need to recognize that the allocation, distribution, and cost of water is the most effective planning tool we have, and we should integrate its management into our land use and development decisions rather than treating it as a separate and distinct question of engineering. The operation, mandate, and function of the Arizona State Land Department should be completely restructured to give it a different sense of accountability and independence, providing a laboratory for best development practices, including open space and desert preservation.

The relationship between municipal tax structure, the use of incentives, and the cost of growth have enormous impact on the shape and character of cities. In Arizona, we tend to rely too much on sales tax as a finance mechanism, often distorting land use patterns. While most of these decisions should continue to be made at the local level, the state should set a framework requiring explicit disclosure of a community's plans for economic development incentives and subsidies. In the Phoenix metropolitan area these plans need regional coordination for consistency and compatible impacts between the various cities.

Personal mobility—including electronic virtual mobility—will continue to be the overwhelmingly dominant transportation pattern in the region, so let us recognize that and figure out how to make things work better. Mass transit systems should be based on flexibility and demand, not on an unrealistic hope of transforming either the shape of the city or the individual behavior patterns of residents. City governments should place far greater emphasis on spreading out the time of daily trips by encouraging telecommuting and should encourage land use patterns that disperse trips to "vital centers" throughout the urban area.

Finally, we have simply grown too large as a metropolis to continue making most land use decisions in a largely ad hoc manner by elected officials. We should follow the lead of other cities in restructuring our development permit process to be primarily plan driven, based on the application of standards, with fewer exceptions for individual parcels and with less political decisions. This means moving away from legislative and toward quasi-judicial decisions.

Step five: Hang on tight and be ready to change

Today we are witnessing the embryonic years of a cultural transformation every bit as profound as that wrought by the rise of the automobile. The auto gave us "sprawl"—the ability to live and work in places connected only by ribbons of pavement, in a lifestyle of unparalleled mobility. As we move from the city on wheels to the city on the wire, working and living patterns have and will change. What our cities will look like when people can plug in and work from home, from Starbucks, from a telecommuting center, and at whatever time is convenient, we cannot yet predict. More density or less? Probably both, since for the first time in human history our urban form will not be dictated principally by the means of available physical transportation.

Phoenix, the prototypical post-industrial city, should be at the forefront of this revolution. Instead of arguing over how to emulate the last generation of cities, we should talk about how to build the future city of choices. This is the trick: not to create artificial development constraints in the hope of either driving people away or forcing them to live in a preordained pattern, but rather to use what regulatory influence we have to encourage a multitude of work and lifestyle alternatives that fit together in patterns protecting what is special about where we live. Our regulatory mechanisms will need constant adjustment to deal with the nature of growth and development, and so flexibility and a willingness to experiment are critical. The future is a process.

Tonight my family and I went to some friends' house in Tempe. They live in a one-story ranch house in a neighborhood built in the early 1960s. The curvy streets are lined mostly with Bermuda grass lawns and palm trees. The original roofs here were shake shingles, a poor material for desert houses, and some owners have replaced theirs with concrete tile. The houses have garages, used brick trim, and slump block. This was a move-up neighborhood, and remains stable, well maintained, and attractive.

Our friends have lived here for a dozen years, as have many of their neighbors. New owners are often ASU faculty, and change the landscaping to designer desert complete with big boulders. There are signs of kids of every age: big wheels, BMX bikes, Honda Civics with chrome tailpipes and low-profile tires.

We drank margaritas, talked about politics, the stock market, and growing old. Our kids played Nintendo to avoid talking to each other. My friend Jerry and I grew up and went away to college together. Another old friend, Bill, joined us. I told them about this book and we talked about how much Tempe and Phoenix have changed since we were all kids. Bill thinks the city is terrible now, full of too many people, ruined by politicians and developers. He's pretty sure I'm at least partly to blame. He wanted to do something radical to stop the growth that's wrecked this place, but now he says it's too late, so he'll move out as soon as he can afford to, fleeing to the mountains. Jerry avoided most of the argument, but at the end said that we can't shut off the growth until after his family sells the 160 acres of desert they've held in north Scottsdale for 15 years.

We worked our way through the evening like that, sitting on the patio.

Notes

Introduction (pages 1–5)

1. Sorkin 1997; Shoumatoff 1997, 368; Adler 1995; Reisner 1986, 1.
2. Ward 1997; Moe 1997; Kunstler 1997.
3. See, for example, Katz 1994; Calthorpe 1993; Duany and Plater-Zyberk 1991.
4. Throughout this book references to Phoenix, greater Phoenix, metropolitan Phoenix, or the Valley of the Sun will generally be used interchangeably. Often statistics will refer to all of Maricopa County. The Phoenix Standard Metropolitan Statistical Area is defined by the U.S. Department of Commerce to include all of Maricopa and Pinal Counties, which works for population statistics, but includes enormous amounts of vacant area. When a reference is intended to indicate only the Phoenix city limits or the government of the City of Phoenix, the term *City of Phoenix* will generally be used.
5. Parts of this paragraph originally appeared in Gammage 1996.

Betting on a Boom (pages 9–20)

1. The Census Bureau noted the disappearance of a contiguous frontier line in the report on the 1890 census.
2. Turner 1963.
3. See Simonson 1963, 12.
4. The best general history of the Phoenix is Bradford Luckingham's *Phoenix: The history of a Southwestern metropolis*. General background on the history of Phoenix in this and subsequent chapters relies heavily on his work.
5. City of Phoenix 1992, 26.
6. Luckingham 1989, 21–22.
7. Moe and Wilkie 1997, 103.
8. Rybczynski 1995, 55. The Spanish, as the original European settlers in the Southwest, had similarly rejected most native traditions, also using a grid to lay out their settlements. Available materials had earlier limited the Spanish to a continued use of adobe.
9. The Desert Land Act of 1877 increased the size to 600 acres, which was more realistic.
10. City of Phoenix 1992, 44.
11. Ryden 1989.
12. Rybczynski 1995, 93.
13. Rybczynski 1995, 109.
14. Luckingham 1989, 81.
15. Shoumatoff 1997, 361–362.
16. Luckingham 1989, 74.
17. So et al. 1988, 251–254.

18. City of Phoenix 1989, 53.

19. City of Phoenix 1992, 63.

20. Hise 1997, 135–136.

21. *Infrastructure,* for these purposes, means sewer, water, and other utilities. The term is also generally inclusive of streets.

22. Clark 1986, 200.

23. Hise 1997, 39 (letter dated 10 January 1924).

24. MacLeish 1932.

25. Hise 1997, 71–72.

26. Luckingham 1989, 107.

27. Luckingham 1989, 135.

28. Hise 1997, 1–13.

Liquid Glue (pages 21–31)

1. Many newspaper accounts of this episode exist, differing in some details. This account is also based on Zarbin 1995.

2. Reisner 1986, 268.

3. Shoumatoff 1997, 29.

4. Zarbin 1997, 86–87. Zarbin's book is an interesting account of the canal building efforts before the Newlands Act.

5. Stegner 1992, 229.

6. Zarbin 1997, 124, 143, 193.

7. In this regard see Zarbin 1997.

8. Heard's relationship with early reclamation efforts often put him at odds with other landowners. At times he challenged the established leadership of what would become the Salt River Project, advocating more localized control and mechanisms to discourage speculative land assemblage. Heard's own interests were actually often better served by positions contrary to those that he advocated, but he was nevertheless criticized in Phoenix for self-interest. His involvement in these early debates is well examined in Smith 1986.

9. Smith 1986, 16–18.

10. On the early history of the SRP, also see Smith 1986.

11. Luckingham 1989, 47.

12. Luckingham 1989, 164.

13. From the outset, the entire system was referred to as the Salt River Project, the term the Bureau of Reclamation had used.

14. Arizona Revised Statutes, §48-2301, et seq.

15. Salt River Project 1998.

16. SRP's role as a shadow government is profiled in Garreau 1991. The one acre/one vote system was upheld as constitutional against a consumer-based lawsuit in *James v. Ball* (451 U.S. 355 [1981]).

17. Interestingly, in the late 1980s, SRP projected full urbanization by

2010. More recent thinking is that there will remain pockets of agriculture, especially in the southwest part of the area. This change is the result of the more recent growth of Phoenix heading north, into the desert. Sources: John Keane and John Sullivan of SRP.

18. The upper basin includes Colorado, Wyoming, New Mexico, Utah, and the portion of Arizona above Lee's Ferry. The lower basin consists of the rest of Arizona, Nevada, and California.

19. An acre-foot of water is the amount necessary to cover one acre of land to a depth of one foot. It is 325,851 gallons, roughly the amount used by a Phoenix family of five in one year.

20. Sheridan 1995, 222–227.

21. Reisner 1986, 270–271, 361–362.

22. Martin 1989, 265–272.

23. Martin 1989, 284.

24. On the CAP generally, see Johnson 1977.

25. Reisner 1986, chapter 9.

26. Luckingham 1989, 203.

27. The original CAP agricultural contracts had included clauses requiring agricultural customers to buy all of the water cities didn't need. These customers defaulted on the contracts and in some cases filed bankruptcy. Ultimately, the contracts were canceled.

28. As of this writing, the dispute is still in litigation, and the parties appear to be about one-half billion dollars apart. The author served as a CAP board member beginning in 1992, and as president of the board from 1994–98. Parts of this narrative are based on personal experience in that capacity.

29. The actual problem was the CAP water's chemistry. As it was different than that of the groundwater that Tucson had used for years, the CAP water caused deposits in the city's pipes to come off. CAP water is drunk throughout Maricopa County without incident.

30. Central Arizona Project 1992–98. In 1993, agricultural delivery was only about 50,000 acre-feet, one-tenth of the previous year's deliveries because of the increase in price required as a result of the notice of completion. By 1994, the CAWCD enacted new pricing policies to lower the cost of agricultural water, and deliveries rebounded to just over half a million acre-feet.

31. Future plans of the Water Banking Authority include allowing California and Nevada to pay for banking water in Arizona. At some point in the future, when those states need to make a "withdrawal," Arizona would pump up the banked water for its own use, and allow the other state to divert an equivalent amount from the main stem of the river.

32. Karl Kohloff, representative of the City of Mesa, quoted in Kammer and Van Der Werf 1998.

33. This can be done, but only at great cost, and then the new area must itself be relatively dense. E.g., Del Webb's new Anthem project on Interstate 17 near New River.

The Industry of Growth (pages 32–48)

1. Luckingham 1989, 84.
2. See Jones 1997, a recently published history of Sky Harbor.
3. Luckingham 1989, 137.
4. Luckingham 1989, 140.
5. Abbott 1993, 26.
6. Bureau of the Census 1951, 522.
7. Phoenix was, in fact, the center of national evaporative cooler manufacturing. The five largest manufacturers together grossed 15 million dollars by 1951. See Cooper 1998.
8. Scheatzle 1998. The credit to Carrier has been widely disputed. Cooper 1998 gives the fullest account. In any event, Carrier is the best known and most popular early tinkerer with air conditioning technology.
9. Jones 1997–98.
10. Cooper 1998, 157.
11. Cooper 1998, 166.
12. In 1957 Robert Barton, a Motorola manager, noted: "We can run an ad in the trade magazines mentioning three places to work, Phoenix, Chicago, and Riverside, California. We'll draw 25 to 1 replies for Phoenix compared with the other cities . . . we don't have to pay a premium to get engineers and other skilled employees to live here, either. The premium is free . . . sunshine." Luckingham 1989, 162.
13. *Arizona Business and Economic Review* June 1954.
14. *The Arizona Republic* May 9 and December 8, 1955. See Luckingham 1989, 161.
15. Luckingham 1989, 159.
16. Venturi et al. 1972; Jackson 1984; Hess 1986.
17. Casazza and Spink 1985, 1.
18. *The Arizona Republic* March 24, 1928.
19. Rybczynski 1995, 201.
20. Casazza and Spink 1985, 12–13.
21. Janus Associates 1984, survey form 262-4. The Publix was torn down in the late 1980s.
22. Casazza and Spink 1985, 16; Rybczynski 1995, 206.
23. Luckingham 1989, 160.
24. Review of 1957 aerial photos at City of Phoenix Historic Preservation Office.
25. Halberstam 1993, 134.

26. Halberstam 1993, 131.
27. Hise 1997, 135.
28. Clark 1986, 201.
29. Clark 1986, 213–215.
30. Peterson 1989.
31. Peterson 1989, 1049.
32. May 1958.
33. Peterson 1989, 1052.
34. City of Phoenix 1992, 101.
35. City of Phoenix 1992, 106–110.
36. Cook 1985.
37. See, generally, Clark 1986, chapter 7. See also Ames 1998.
38. Halberstam 1993, chapter 9.
39. *House and Home* 1961.
40. *House and Home* 1957, 117–118.
41. *American Builder* 1958, 75.
42. *Congressional Record* 1959, 306.
43. Long 1997.
44. Clark 1986, 229.
45. Clark 1986.
46. Reed 1954, 24–29, 38.

Careful What You Wish For (pages 49–59)
1. Bureau of the Census 1998a.
2. Gober 1998.
3. Sheridan 1995, 319.
4. Dunfee 1997.
5. Nilsson 1985 chronicles the history of the Papago inner loop.
6. Nilsson 1985.
7. Luckingham 1989, 201.
8. Dunfee 1997.
9. Luckingham 1989, 193.
10. The early 1974 date is based on the recollections of participants in the meeting and members of the Phoenix Planning Department's staff.
11. The village plan was first formally adopted as the *Concept 2000* plan on July 31, 1979.
12. Downs 1994, 206–210.
13. Garreau 1991, chapter 6. Hise also chronicles the rise of official recognition for multiple cores in Los Angeles, noting that as early as 1944 L.A. had a master plan showing a number of "nuclei" for urbanization.
14. Luckingham 1989, 237.
15. In one controversial zoning case in 1981, the developers of the Phelps

Dodge building at Central Avenue and Virginia Avenue actually hired international solar energy expert John Yellott to model the reflective impact of the building on an adjoining neighborhood. The design of the building incorporated protruding vertical fins between the window panes. The fins were designed to shade the building's windows for the benefit of tenants, but had the effect of breaking up the reflection of heat and light around the building as well, and were dubbed "solar fins" as a result.

16. Binstein and Bowden 1993.

17. Laing 1988.

18. Sheridan 1995, 333.

19. Bureau of the Census 1998b.

To Sprawl or Not to Sprawl (pages 63–74)

1. Quoted in Sahagun 1995.

2. Jacksonville's jurisdictional limits, as of 1990, were 758 square miles. Anchorage, Alaska, is often shown as covering an area of 1,700 square miles. Schmittroth 1998.

3. Whyte 1958.

4. See, for example, the debates between Gordon and Richardson and Reid Ewing, and subsequent correspondence, in the *Journal of the American Planning Association*, Winter and Spring, 1997. For web sites, see www. plannersweb.com; www.bankamerica.com; www.governing.com.

5. Clawson 1962.

6. Guillory et al. 1998.

7. Rybczynski 1995, 226.

8. Kunstler 1993.

9. It is nearly impossible to list all the social ills attributed to "sprawl," or the various articles examining and attacking the phenomenon. For an excellent review of a small fraction of the literature, see Burchell 1997.

10. Longstreth 1995.

11. Fulton 1996, 9.

12. Kopytoff 1996, 26y.

13. There are, to be sure, some exceptions, but they tend to be retirement communities or other developments in which a huge infrastructure investment made it possible for a major planned development to be built in relative isolation.

14. Various sources have claimed that central Phoenix has as much as 35 to 40 percent of its land sitting vacant. Former mayor Terry Goddard, for example, cites this statistic as an example of why "infill" development strategies could provide a major alternative to continued growth on the urban edge. The city's planning department is attempting to develop a comprehensive data base on vacant parcels. Preliminary data from that project

paints a very different picture. In the designated "infill" study area of central Phoenix, which covers 96,000 acres, about 10 percent (9,652 acres) was identified as vacant in 1995. There are, of course, additional parcels that could clearly be viewed as underdeveloped, but quantifying such a statistic is highly subjective.

15. Clawson 1962.

16. Phoenix Historic Preservation Commission 1996.

17. Gordon and Richardson 1997a, 103. Similarly, Burchell 1997 contrasts "sprawl" and "planned development or managed growth." His definition of "sprawl" is of one-third to one-acre lots, floor area ratios of strip commercial below .20. Neither of these applies to most of Phoenix.

18. These statistics are from Gordon and Richardson 1997b. Gordon and Richardson are "defenders" of sprawl—or at least of a relatively free-market-oriented approach to managing growth and city form. Like any set of density statistics, these numbers are entirely dependent on the denominator: how large an area is being averaged, and what is included.

19. Bureau of the Census 1962, 1993.

20. See, e.g, Baron 1998, 100. See also Chris Gehlker quoted in Padgett 1998, 8.

21. Portland's UGB stems from Goal 14, the Urbanization Goal, adopted by the Oregon Land Conservation Development Commission in 1974. The UGB has been managed since 1974 by Portland Metro, the elected regional governance authority (Metro is at 600 NE Grand Ave., Portland, OR 97232). A small sample of the articles on the Portland system include Ehrenhalt 1997 and Claiborne 1997. A comparison with Phoenix appeared in Ingley 1998.

22. Some of the discussion here on UGBs appeared in Gammage 1998.

23. In 1900 Portland had about 90,000 people. By 1930 it had grown to 300,000. In 1990, it was up to 440,000. Phoenix, by contrast, grew from 5,000 people in 1900, to 50,000 in 1930 to just under 1,000,000 in 1990. Portland became a city before the auto was dominant, and therefore had an intense downtown core.

24. See Claiborne 1997 quoting Metro planners' desire to see lot sizes shrink and densities rise. Ehrenhalt 1997 also chronicles the local tensions over increased density projections in suburbs within the Portland UGB.

25. Anthony Downs recognizes this dilemma: "Serious growth-related crises are most likely to arise in metropolitan areas that have two traits simultaneously: they are very large (more than two million inhabitants) and their populations are growing rapidly. But these same traits would make it extremely difficult to maintain rigid urban growth boundaries drawn tightly around the periphery of built-up areas. Where rapid growth is occurring, such tight boundaries would soon require significant increases in residential

densities in built-up neighborhoods. But attempts to increase residential densities there would provoke hostile political reactions from residents. Thus the very conditions most likely to cause political acceptance of this vision would also generate intense resistance to it." Downs 1994, 196.
26. The South Carolina Coastal Commission made (and lost) a similar argument in *Lucas v. South Carolina Coastal Commission*, 112 S. Ct. 2886 (1992). Mr. Lucas's beachfront lots were declared to lie seaward of a baseline prohibiting construction of anything more intense than a viewing or camping deck. The U.S. Supreme Court found that this so severely diminished his property value as to be a total taking of his property, for which the state owed him compensation.
27. Abbott 1993, 125–126.
28. Riley 1967, 23.
29. Luckingham 1989, 233.

City by Choice (pages 75–83)
1. Hill 1992.
2. Wright 197-; Zygas and Johnson 1995.
3. March 1995.
4. Soleri 1969.
5. Wright 197-, 87.
6. See Marlin 1986.
7. Marlin 1986 places Phoenix highest of all U.S. cities in owner-occupied dwellings, exceeded only by four Australian cities.
8. Mitchell 1995.
9. Entrepreneurs are already targeting this market. Examples include Boston Market, Emily's Market, Oscar's, and Foodini.
10. Mitchell 1995 points out the synchronous/asynchronous dichotomy, among many others.
11. Mitchell 1995, 96; 1997 statistic from the Institute for the Study of Distrib-uted Work, see Goluboff 1998, xix.
12. *The Business Journal* November 7, 1997, 14B.
13. Stanséll 1995.
14. Henton and Walesh 1998.

Limits to Growth (pages 84–93)
1. Adler 1995.
2. Hayward and VonDohlen 1996.
3. Greater Phoenix Economic Council 1996, 64.
4. Gammage 1996.
5. Arizona Department of Water Resources 1991.
6. In fact, based on current and projected population trends, an even higher

percentage of the urban population of the three counties is likely to be in Maricopa.

7. Greater Phoenix Economic Council 1996, 76.

8. Arizona Department of Water Resources as quoted in Greater Phoenix Economic Council 1996.

9. Luckingham 1989, 247.

10. Parsons Brinckerhoff Quade & Douglas, Inc. 1994.

11. In 1995, ozone concentrations exceeded federal standards eleven times, carbon monoxide three times, and particulates twice. In 1997, the only violations were ozone on two days. See Morrison Institute for Public Policy 1998a. In the mid-1980s, the Valley experienced carbon monoxide violations between 45 and 90 times each year. Maricopa Association of Governments 1998.

12. E.g., The Morrison Institute for Public Policy 1998a quality of life indicators cite 88 percent of the public as perceiving the quality of air to be fair or poor.

13. Lougeay et al. 1996.

14. The urban heat island phenomenon is being studied in a number of urban areas, including Atlanta, Sacramento, Los Angeles, and Salt Lake City. This phenomenon may well be an additional reason why drawing a noose around the urban area to force higher densities is not the best planned solution to future growth. Intermixed large areas of preserved open space could act as climatic moderators in our giant experiment in weather modification.

15. Yozwiak 1998, citing the work of Robert Balling, director of the Office of Climatology at Arizona State University.

16. "Hottest" as a phenomenon is susceptible to different definitions. On a mean annual average temperature basis, tropical, not desert, cities rank highest since their range of temperature is narrow. But when defined by average temperature in midsummer (July in the northern hemisphere), Phoenix has been ranked second only to Manama, Nicaragua. Marlin 1986, 518.

17. Professor Balling doesn't agree: "I don't think it's going to be a limiting factor at all. I do not believe people are going to stop moving to Phoenix because it's too darn hot here." Quoted in Yozwiak 1998.

18. Hardin 1968.

19. See, generally, Kelly 1993.

20. Maricopa Association of Governments 1998.

21. The analysis of available water for growth is complicated by the concept of "priority" built into water allocations. While the CAP canal can deliver 1.5 MAF on average to central Arizona, less than half of that (640,000 acre-feet) is classified as having a municipal and industrial (M&I) priority. M&I priority means that that water is highly reliable and that in times of

shortage, its delivery would take precedent over agricultural priority water. The fixing of such priorities is done by the Secretary of the Interior, based partly on the best available estimates of historical flows of the Colorado River, but also partly on political factors. The Arizona Water Banking Authority was established in 1996 as a mechanism to store Colorado River water in the underground aquifers within Arizona. In its first two years of operation, the authority stored about 260,000 acre-feet in Maricopa County. That stored water may be called upon in times of shortage to further supplement M&I supplies, thereby making lower priority water more reliable.

22. The Del Webb Corporation, for example, entered into a long-term lease of water allocated to the Ak-Chin tribe in order to secure a source for its Anthem development near New River. An earlier example of water flowing toward urban populations was the "water farm" marketing of the 1980s. Cities in Maricopa County were acquiring huge tracts of agricultural land in outlying counties in order to retire the land from agriculture and use either the water located there (moved by canal) or the paper water rights (moved by exchange) to the Phoenix area, a maneuver reminiscent of Los Angeles's purchase of the Owens Valley. In response to concerns by the rural counties that their economies would be undermined by these efforts, the legislature put a halt to such possible transfers.

23. Weinberg 1997.

24. Western Water Policy Review Advisory Commission 1998.

25. For example, California has adopted a series of farmland preservation preferential tax assessments since the mid-1960s, starting with the California Land Conservation Act (The Williamson Act) Cal. Gov. Code §51200-295.

26. Just as even Portland's UGB can be moved—and recently was.

27. The best known sources on the worldwide shortage of potable water are the writings of Postel, including *The Last Oasis*.

Save the Desert (pages 97–103)

1. Dunbier 1968, 4; Bender 1982.

2. The term "designer deserts" was coined by Bruce Berger in *The Telling Distance*, 1997.

3. Berger 1997.

4. Using arid plants to xeriscape a subdivision yard is not a bad thing. I live in a house with such landscaping, and in the new areas where we are building in the desert, it is appropriate to at least discourage, maybe even prohibit, front yards from having grass and non-desert trees and shrubs. But such landscaped versions of the desert do not satisfy the demand for preservation of actual desert. We also should recognize that the context of most Valley neighborhoods before the 1980s was not development of the desert,

but rather of farmland. Those subdivisions exist in the irrigated oasis part of the valley, and their landscaping should retain that character, not be retro-fitted with designer deserts.

5. MAG 1996.

Community as Commodity (pages 104–113)

Portions of this chapter appeared earlier as Gammage 1996.

1. These are actual paint colors, all in the range of "beige."

2. It is difficult to obtain hard statistics on this change. Various builders and knowledgeable observers, when asked to date the change, give a range from 1978 to 1982.

3. Walsh 1998.

4. For the first quarter of 1998, Phoenix ranked 122 in the country in housing affordability. This compares to San Francisco's 191, San Jose's 185, San Diego's 177, Los Angeles's 171, and Orange County's 167. See Colburn 1998.

5. Walsh 1998. Nationally, in 1971 73 percent of homes built were one story. In 1996, single-story housing starts dropped below 50 percent.

6. Trunnelle 1997.

7. Harvey 1975.

8. Mumford 1961, 490–495.

9. E.g., see Riesman 1950; Keats 1959; and Wood 1959.

10. See Gammage 1991, 1994.

11. I was the chair of the DRSC as this process evolved, and most of the account comes directly from that experience.

12. For example, in R-1-6, the maximum density is five units to the acre, rather than the previously permitted 5.3.

13. Text amendment 9-97.

14. See Gammage 1991, 1994.

15. See Gammage 1994.

16. *The Arizona Republic* 1998a.

17. E.g., see *The Wall Street Journal* 1998.

In Trust (pages 114–120)

1. Gammage and Schroeder 1989.

2. Gammage and Schroeder 1989.

3. Many developers hoped the preference would act like a right of first refusal, thereby discouraging others from bidding. A developer holding a preference would combine it with the planning permit to plan the land as if it was under option or in escrow subject to zoning.

4. Gammage and Schroeder 1989.

5. The statute is ARS§37-335(C); the lawsuit was Ewing v. State of Arizona 745 P2d 947 (Az. App. 1987).

6. *Gladden Farms v. State of Arizona* 633 P2d 325 (Az. 1981).

7. *Fain Land and Cattle Co. v. Hassell* 790 P2d 242 (Az. 1990).

8. This proposed change in structure will likely require a constitutional amendment, which could be packaged on the ballot with amendments permitting limited exchange authority and explicitly allowing the department to facilitate preservation of open space.

Getting Around (pages 121–127)

1. Waits and Johnson 1996.

2. Downs 1994.

3. World Resources Institute 1996, 83.

4. ULI 1989.

5. VonDohlen 1996.

6. Dunfee 1997.

7. The Curitiba transit system is being promoted in the United States by the Surface Transportation Project, 434 South Plymouth Boulevard, Los Angeles, California, Martha Welborne, Project Director. Orlando, Los Angeles, and Eugene, Oregon, are planning such systems.

8. Wood 1998.

Paying for Growth (pages 128–136)

1. Burchell 1997.

2. See, e.g., Gordon and Richardson 1997a. This article resulted in a response, Ewing 1997, and a reply in Gordon and Richardson 1997b.

3. Black 1996.

4. Guhathakurta and Wichert 1988.

5. Burchell 1997, 160.

6. Burchell 1997, 167–169.

7. See, e.g., Nicholas et al. 1991.

8. In 1998 the legislature finally passed an education finance reform package, which was approved by the Arizona Supreme Court. The system will alleviate the rich/poor disparity, and may help the fast-growth problem because of a new state construction fund. The fund is woefully inadequate, however, and many fast-growing districts believe that their needs will continue to go unmet. Mean-while, most of the development community is opposed to education impact fees because they believe they will be excessively charged, and their residents will effectively wind up paying for new schools both in their home price (which is were impact fees are repaid) and in their property tax bills.

9. ARS§42-681, *et seq.*, repealed 1995.

10. ARS§42-1901, *et seq.*

11. The best study on the use of incentives in Arizona, particularly for

industrial employment type uses, remains Waits and Katler 1993. This study proposes a comprehensive series of questions that should be asked before incentives would be offered, and analyzes policies of "competing" states. The study is focused on jobs and statewide policy, and therefore does not deal at length with local retail and redevelopment policies, which have a greater impact on land use patterns.

12. This attitude is in stark and intriguing contrast to that of the State of Oregon, which has a historic antipathy toward the sales tax. This attitudinal difference has major implications for urban form and development. Cities in Arizona vie with one another to put big box retail on their edges in order to derive revenue from an adjoining jurisdiction. Thus, limiting peripheral growth is much more difficult in a sales-tax driven government climate.

And the Process Is the Substance (pages 137–143)

1. The zoning hearing recounted here is not real, but rather is the synthesis of dozens of similar cases. The names are similarly fabricated.

2. The leading case imposing quasi-judicial standards is *Fasano v. Board of County Commissioners*, 507 P2d 23 (Or., 1973); in Washington, *Smith v. Skagit Co.*, 453 P2d 832 (Wa., 1969) reached the same result, adopting an appearance of fairness doctrine. Both cases are revealing in demonstrating the discomfort of judges in reviewing the free-for-all of city council zoning decisions. Numerous commentators have urged a move toward rezoning decisions being quasi-judicial, and that posture was endorsed by the American Law Institute's 1975 model development code and by a 1978 ABA commission.

3. Changing to a more plan-driven quasi-judicial zoning process may not be appropriate in smaller, more isolated communities where the city council, acting in a legislative capacity, should review every land use issue. In the Phoenix metropolitan area, it is time for fewer ad hoc decisions.

4. Chapter 204, Laws 1998, Forty-third Legislature, Second Regular Session.

5. Similar changes are made to the county zoning and planning enabling acts.

6. Unfortunately, a recent case confirms Arizona's long-standing view that rezonings are legislative and general plans largely meaningless. See *Fritz v. City of Kingman*, 957 P2d 337 (Az., 1998).

7. The number is currently set by the Arizona Constitution at 10 percent of the qualified electors of a city town or county, Article 4, Part 1, Sec. 1(9). The constitution defines the term *qualified electors* for statewide matters as being those who voted in the last election of the governor. Statutes (ARS Sec. 19-142) define qualified electors in the local context to be those who voted in the last election at which a mayor or councilmembers were elected. Because local election turnout is so low, the number for a referendum is absurd. The required number should be pegged at 10 percent of registered

voters. This change may be possible by amending only the statute, or may require a constitutional amendment.

Conclusion (pages 144–150)

1. City of Phoenix 1998; Morrison Institute for Public Policy 1998a.
2. Jacobs 1961.
3. In City of Phoenix 1998, 72 percent found quality of life in the city to be excellent to good. Morrison Institute for Public Policy 1998a put the same statistic at 67 percent on a regional basis.
4. See, for example, Morrison Institute for Public Policy 1998a, 10–11.
5. Adler and Springen 1998.

Bibliography

Abbott, Carl. 1993. *The metropolitan frontier: Cities in the modern American West*. Tucson: The University of Arizona Press.

Adler, Jerry. 1995. Bye-bye, suburban dream. *Newsweek* May 15.

Adler, Jerry, and Karen Springen. 1998. Back at the ranch. *Newsweek* October 12, 58–59.

American Builder. 1958. Here's a $9500 best seller in America's top growth area. June: 74–75.

Ames, David. 1998. Context and guidelines for evaluating America's historic suburbs for the National Register of Historic Places. Unpublished draft available from the Center for Historic Architecture and Design, University of Delaware, Newark, Delaware.

Arizona Business and Economic Review. 1954. Motorola expands in Phoenix. June: 1–2.

Arizona Department of Water Resources. 1991. *Management plan for the second management period, 1990–2000*. Phoenix: Arizona Department of Water Resources.

The Arizona Republic. 1928. Seventh of Bayless chain gorcery store opens: Investment of $60,000 put in establishment. March 24, section 2 page 1.

———. 1955b. Phoenix must grow. May 9, section 1 page 6.

———. 1955a. Phoenix or Scottsdale? December 8, section 1 page 6.

———. 1998. Home cost outgains income. February 25.

Arizona Revised Statutes, §48-2301, et seq.

Banham, Reyner. 1971. *Los Angeles: The architecture of four ecologies*. New York: Harper & Row.

Baron, David. 1998. Initiative gives voters control over growth. In *Growth in Arizona: The machine in the garden*. Tempe: Morrison Institute for Public Policy, Arizona State University.

Bender, Gordon, ed. 1982. *Reference handbook on the deserts of North America*. Westport, Conn.: Greenwood Press.

Berger, Bruce. 1997. *The telling distance*. Tucson: University of Arizona Press.

Binstein, Michael, and Charles Bowden. 1993. *Trust me: Charles Keating and the missing billions*. New York: Random House.

Black, J. Thomas. 1996. Commentary: The economics of sprawl. *Urban Land* 55(3): 6, 52.

Burchell, Robert W. 1997. Economic and fiscal costs (and benefits) of sprawl. *The Urban Lawyer* 29(2): 159–181.

Bureau of the Census. 1951. *Statistical abstract of the United States*. Washington, D.C.: U.S. Department of Commerce, Economics and Statistics Administration, Bureau of the Census.

———. 1962. *County and city bata book: 1962*. Washington, D.C.: U.S. Department of Commerce, Economics, and Statistics Administration.

———. 1993a. *1990 census of population and housing: Arizona.* Washington, D.C.: U.S. Department of Commerce, Economics, and Statistics Administration.

———. 1993b. *1990 census of population and housing: California.* Washington, D.C.: U.S. Department of Commerce, Economics, and Statistics Administration.

———. 1993c. *1990 census of population and housing: New York* Washington, D.C.: U.S. Department of Commerce, Economics, and Statistics Administration.

———. 1998a. *State and metropolitan area data book 1997–98.* 5th edition. Washington, D.C.: U.S. Department of Commerce, Economics, and Statistics Administration.

———. 1998b. *U.S. census of construction industries: Housing units authorized by building permits.* Washington, D.C.: U.S. Department of Commerce, Economics, and Statistics Administration.

The Business Journal. 1997. Chart of greater Phoenix employment, August 1997. November 7, 14B.

Calthorpe, Peter. 1993. *The next American metropolis: Ecology, community, and the American dream.* New York: Princeton Archtiectural Press.

Casazza, John A., and Frank H. Spink Jr. 1985. *Shopping center development handbook.* 2nd ed. Washington, D.C.: The Urban Land Institute.

City of Phoenix. 1989. *The WILLO-Alvarado multiple property area: Historic resources survey.* Phoenix: Planning Department.

———. 1992. *Historic homes of Phoenix: An architectural and preservation guide.* Phoenix: City of Phoenix.

———. 1998. *Community attitude survey.* Phoenix: City of Phoenix.

Claiborne, William. 1997. Cracks in the great wall of Portland. *Washington Post*, national weekly edition, October 6, 32.

Clark, Clifford Edward. 1986. *The American family home, 1800–1960.* Chapel Hill: University of North Carolina Press.

Clawson, Marion. 1962. Urban sprawl and speculation in suburban land. *Land Economics* 38(2): 99.

Colburn, Andrea. 1998. Housing opporuntiy index-first quarter 1998. Housing Economics June.

Congressional Record. 1959. Housing Act of 1959. Washington, D.C.

Cook, Jeffrey. 1985. Contrasting house prototypes: The Arab atrium houses versus the U.S. ranch houses. *Arid lands today and tomorrow: Proceedings of an international research and development conference, Tucson, Arizona, USA, October 20–25, 1985.* Boulder, Colo.: Westview Press.

Cooper, Gail. 1998. *Air conditioning America: Engineers and the controlled environment 1900–1960*. Baltimore: Johns Hopkins University Press.

Downs, Anthony. 1994. *New visions for metropolitan America*. Washington, D.C. : Brookings Institution.

Duany, Andres, and Elizabeth Plater-Zyberk. 1991. *Towns and town-making principles*. New York: Rizzoli.

Dunbier, Roger. 1968. *The Sonoran Desert: Its geography, economy, and people*. Tucson: University of Arizona Press.

Dunphy, Robert. 1997. Passing gridlock. *Urban Land* November 56(7): 39–42, 68.

Ehrenhalt, Alan. 1997. The great wall of Portland. *Governing* May: 20–24.

Ewing v. State of Arizona, 745 P2d 947 (Az. App. 1987).

Ewing, Reid. 1997. Is Los Angeles-style sprawl desirable? *Journal of the American Planning Association* 63(1): 107–126.

Fain Land and Cattle Co. v. Hassell, 790 P2d 242 (1990).

Fasano v. Board of County Commissioners, 507 P2d 23 (Or., 1973).

Fleming, Lawrence J. 1977. *Ride a mile and smile the while: A history of the Phoenix Street Railway, 1887–1948*. Phoenix: Swaine Publications.

Fritz v. City of Kingman, 957 P2d 337 (Az., 1998).

Fulton, William. 1996. *The new urbanism*. Cambridge, Mass.: Lincoln Institute of Land Policy.

Gammage, Grady Jr. 1991. Phoenix does it citywide. *Planning* 57(5): 15–17.

———. 1994. Design review comes to Phoenix. In Design review: Challenging urban aesthetic control, edited by Brenda Case Scheer and Wolfgang F. E. Presier. New York: Chapman and Hall.

———. 1996. Growing weary? *Phoenix Magazine* November: 104–117.

———. 1998. Thoughts on urban growth boundaries. *Arizona Planning* February: 1, 10–11.

Gammage, Grady Jr., and Karen L. Schroeder. 1989. The bureaucrat as developer: Arizona's Urban Lands Act. *Urban Land* 48(2): 11–15.

Garreau, Joel. 1991. *Edge city: Life on the new frontier*. New York: Doubleday.

Gladden Farms v. State of Arizona, 633 P2d 325 (1981).

Gober, Patricia. 1998. The demographics of urban growth in Phoenix. In *Growth in Arizona: The machine in the garden*. Tempe: Morrison Institute for Public Policy, Arizona State University.

Gordon, Peter, and Harry Richardson. 1997a. Are compact cities a desirable planning goal? *Journal of the American Planning Association* 63(1): 95–106.

———. 1997b. Letter to the editor: Where's the sprawl? *Journal of the American Planning Association* 63(2): 275–278.

Goluboff, Nicole Belson. 1998. *Telecommuting for lawyers*. Chicago:

American Bar Association.

Greater Phoenix Economic Council. 1996. *Greater Phoenix by the numbers*. Phoenix: Greater Phoenix Economic Council.

Guhathakurta, Subhrajit, and Michele L. Wichert. 1998. Who pays for growth in the city of Phoenix? *Urban Affairs Review* 33(6): 813–839.

Guillory, Renee, et al. 1998. *Sprawl costs us all: A citizen's guide to the hidden costs of sprawl and what we can do to grow responsibly.* Phoenix: Sierra Club Grand Canyon Chapter and Southwest Office.

Halberstam, David.1993. *The fifties.* New York: Villard Books.

Hardin, Garrett. 1968. Tragedy of the commons. *Science* 162: 1243–1248.

Harvey, David. 1975. A social critic's perspective. In *The manipulated city: Perspectives on spatial structure and social issues in urban America,* edited by Stephen Gale and Eric G. Moore. Chicago: Maaroufa Press.

Hayward, Steve, and Eric VonDohlen. 1996. *Growth in the Phoenix area: A primer on policy choices.* Arizona Issue Analysis 137. Phoenix: Goldwater Institute.

Henton, Douglas, and Kimberly Walesh. 1998. *The new economy and growth.* A report for the James Irvine Foundation. Reprint. Tempe: The Morrison Institute, Arizona State University.

Hess, Alan. 1986. *Googie: Fifties coffee shop architecture.* San Francisco, Calif.: Chronicle Books.

Hill, David R. 1992. America's disorganized organists. *Journal of Planning Literature* 7(1): 3–21.

Hise, Greg. 1997. Magnetic Los Angeles: Planning the twentieth-century metropolis. Baltimore: Johns Hopkins University Press.

House and Home. 1957. How to start a one-man boom: The John Long story. February: 116–131.

———. 1961. Bill Levitt and John Long. December: 119–129.

Howard, Ebenezer. 1965. *Garden cities of to-morrow.* First published 1898. Cambridge, Mass.: MIT press.

Ingley, Kathleen. 1998. Urban growth boundaries are key point in effort to control Valley's growth: Where Portland draws the line. *The Arizona Republic* May 17, section A page 1.

Jackson, J. B. 1984. *Discovering the vernacular landscape.* New Haven, Conn.: Yale University Press.

Jacobs, Jane. 1961. *The death and life of great American cities.* New York: Vintage Books.

James v. Ball (451 U.S. 355 [1981]).

Janus Associates. 1984. *Historic Phoenix commercial property survey.* Phoenix: Junior League of Phoenix, Inc.

Johnson, Rich. 1977. *The Central Arizona Project, 1918–1968.* Tucson: University of Arizona Press.

Jones, Malcolm Jr. 1997–98. Air conditioning. *Newsweek, extra edition 2000: New millenium, the power of invention* Winter: 42–43.

Jones, Michael D. 1997. *Desert wings: A history of Phoenix Sky Harbor International Airport.* Tempe, Ariz.: Jetblast Publications.

Kammer, Jerry, and Martin Van Der Werf. 1998 Water is our birthright. *The Arizona Republic* February 6, section B: 1–2.

Katz, Peter. 1994. *The new urbanism: Toward an architecture of community.* New York: McGraw-Hill.

Keats, John. 1959. *The crack in the picture window.* Boston: Houghton Mifflin.

Kelly, Eric D. 1993. *Managing community growth: Policies, techniques, and impacts.* Westport, Conn.: Praeger.

Kopytoff, Verne. 1996. Sprawling Phoenix getting a downtown. *New York Times* May 26.

Kunstler, James Howard. 1993. *The geography of nowhere: The rise and decline of America's man-made landscape.* New York: Simon & Schuster.

Laing, Jonathon. 1988. Phoenix descending: Is boomtown going bust? *Barron's* December 19.

Long, John F. 1997. Interview with the author. April.

Longstreth, Richard. 1995. I can't see it; I don't understand it; and it doesn't look old to me. *Historic Preservation Forum* 10(1): 6–15.

Lougeay, Ray, Anthony Brazel, and Mark Hubble. 1996. Monitoring intraurban temperature patterns and associated land cover in Phoenix, Arizona, using Landsat thermal data. *Geocarto International* 11(4): 79–90.

Lucas v. South Carolina Coastal Commission, 112 S. Ct. 2886 (1992).

Luckingham, Bradford. 1989. *Phoenix: The history of a Southwestern metropolis.* Tucson: University of Arizona Press.

MacLeish, Archibald. 1932. *Housing America, by the editors of Fortune.* New York: Harcourt Brace.

March, Lionel. 1995 Broadacre City: Intellectual sources. In *Frank Lloyd Wright: The Phoenix papers*, volume I, edited by K. Paul Zygas. Tempe: Herberger Center for Design Excellence, Arizona State University.

Maricopa Association of Governments. 1996. *Desert spaces: An open space plan for the Maricopa Asso-ciation of Governments.* Phoenix: Maricopa Association of Governments.

———. 1998. The home we share. Handouts provided at the Valley Vision 2025 Citizens' Summit, Orpheum Theatre, June 6.

Marlin, John Tepper. 1986. *Book of world city rankings.* New York: Free Press.

Martin, Russell. 1989. *A story that stands like a dam: Glen Canyon and the struggle for the soul of the West.* New York: Holt.

May, Cliff. 1958. *Western ranch houses.* Menlo Park, Calif.: Lane.

Mitchell, William J. 1995. *City of bits: Space, place, and the infobahn.* Cambridge, Mass.: MIT Press.

Moe, Richard. 1997. *Growing smarter: Fighting sprawl and restoring community in America.* Washington, D.C.: National Trust for Historic Preservation.

Moe, Richard, and Carter Wilkie. 1997. *Changing places: Rebuilding community in the age of sprawl.* New York: Henry Holt.

Morrison Institute for Public Policy. 1998a. *What matters in greater Phoenix: Indicators of our quality of life.* Tempe: Morrison Institute for Public Policy, Arizona State University.

————. 1998b. *Growth in Arizona: The machine in the garden.* Tempe: Morrison Institute for Public Policy, Arizona State University.

Mumford, Lewis. 1961. *The city in history: Its origins, its transformations, and its prospects.* New York: Harcourt, Brace and World.

Nicholas, James C., Arthur C. Nelson, and Julian C. Juergensmeyer. 1991. *A practitioner's guide to development impact fees.* Chicago: American Planning Association.

Nilsson, Joel. 1985. Road to oblivion: Papago put Phoenix on the path of freeway extinction. *The Arizona Republic.* March 24, section C page 1.

Padgett, Mike. 1998. Gowth pains: Solutions key to future. *The Phoenix Business Journal* April 24.

Parsons Brinckerhoff Quade & Douglas, Inc. 1994. *Congestion management system alternatives: Final report.* Phoenix: Maricopa Association of Governments.

Peterson, Gary G. 1989. Home off the range: The origins and evolution of ranch style architecture in the United States. *Design Methods and Theories* 23(3): 1040–1059.

Phoenix Business Journal. 1997. Top 50 Homebuilders. August 15.

Phoenix Historic Preservation Commission. 1996. *Ten vital years in the history of Phoenix.* Phoenix: City of Phoenix.

Postel, Sandra. 1977. *The last oasis: Facing water scarcity.* New York: Worldwatch Institute.

Reed, Allen C. 1954. Dream homes by the dozen. *Arizona Highways* September: 24–29, 38–39.

Reisner, Marc. 1986. *Cadillac desert: The American West and its disappearing water.* New York: Viking.

Riesman, David. 1950. *The lonely crowd: A study of the changing American character.* New Haven, Conn.: Yale University Press.

Riley, Robert. 1967. Urban myths and the new cities of the Southwest. *Landscape Magazine* 17(1): 21–23.

Rybczynski, Witold. 1995. *City life: Urban expectations in a new world.* New York: Touchstone.

Ryden, Don. 1989 *South Mountain agricultural area: Historic resources survey*. Phoenix: Ryden Architects.

Sahagun, Louis. 1995. How Phoenix got so hot. *LA Times Magazine* December 24.

Salt River Project. 1998. *1997 annual report*. Phoenix: Salt River Project.

Scheatzle, David. 1998. Interview with research assistant.

Schmittroth, Linda. 1998. *Cities of the United States*. 3d ed. Detroit, Mich.: Gale Research Inc.

Sheridan, Thomas E. 1995. *Arizona: A history*. Tucson: University of Arizona Press.

Shoumatoff, Alex. 1997. *Legends of the American desert: Sojourns in the greater Southwest*. New York: Knopf.

Simonson, Harold P. 1963. Foreword to *The Significance of the Frontier in American History*, by Frederick Jackson Turner. New York: Frederick Ungar Publishing Company.

Smith, Karen L. 1986. *The magnificent experiment: Building the Salt River reclamation project*. Tucson: University of Arizona Press.

Smith v. Skagit Co., 453 P2d 832 (Wa., 1969).

So, Frank S., and Judith Getzels, eds. 1988. The practice of local government planning. Washington, D.C. : Published for the ICMA Training Institute by the International City Management Association.

Soleri, Paolo. 1969. *Arcology: The city in the image of man*. Cambridge, Mass.: MIT Press.

Sorkin, Michael. 1997. Can Williams and Tsien's Phoenix Art Museum help this sprawling desert city find its edge? *Architectural Record* 1: 83–97.

Stanséll, Kimberly. 1995. Home-based havens. *Home Office Computing* December: 73–78.

Stegner, Wallace. 1992. *Beyond the hundredth meridian: John Wesley Powell and the second opening of the West*. Originally published 1954. New York: Penguin Books.

Trunnelle, Judy. 1997. Top 50 homebuilders in the Valley. Phoenix Business Journal August 15.

Turner, Frederick Jackson. 1963. The significance of the frontier in American history. Edited by Harold W. Simonson. Paper first presented 1893. New York: Frederick Ungar Publishing Company.

ULI. 1989. *Myths and facts about transportation and growth*. Washington, D.C.: The Urban Land Institute.

Venturi, Robert, Denise Scott Brown, and Steven Izenour. 1972. *Learning from Las Vegas*. Cambridge, Mass.: MIT Press.

VonDohlen, Eric. 1996. *Growth, "quality of life" and metropolitan comparisons*. Arizona Issue Analysis 142. Phoenix: Goldwater Institute.

Waits, Mary Jo, and Ryan M. Johnson. 1996. *Transit in the Valley: Where do we go from here?* Tempe: Morrison Institute for Public Policy, Arizona State University.

Waits, Mary Jo, and Marcie Katler. 1993. *Comparative analysis and guidelines for an Arizona incentive policy.* Tempe: Morrison Institute for Public Policy, Arizona State University.

The Wall Street Journal. 1998. A house for the new millenium. August 7.

Walsh, Michael. 1998. Grand homes may not be greatest homes. *The Arizona Republic* June 13.

Ward, Greg. 1997. *Southwest USA.* London: Rough Guides.

Weinberg, Marca. 1997. *Water use conflicts in the West: Implications of reforming the Bureau of Reclamation's water supply policies.* Washington, D.C.: Congressional Budget Office.

Western Water Policy Review Advisory Commission. 1998. *Water in the West: The challenge for the next century, report of the Western Water Policy Review Advisory Commission.* Denver, Colo.: Western Water Policy Review Advisory Commission.

Wood, Daniel B. 1998. 'Fun' is new mortar of a rebuilt Phoenix. *Christian Science Monitor* June 1, page 1.

Wood, Robert Coldwell. 1959. *Suburbia: Its people and their politics.* Boston: Houghton Mifflin.

World Resources Institute. 1996. *World resources: A report by the World Resources Institute and the International Institute for Environment and Development.* New York: Oxford University Press.

Wright, Frank Lloyd. 197-. *The living city: An introduction to Broadacre City: Frank Lloyd Wright, architect.* [unknown]: Frank Lloyd Wright Foundation.

Whyte, William H. Jr. 1958. Urban sprawl. In *The exploding metropolis by the editors of Fortune.* Garden City, N.Y.: Anchor Books.

Yozwiak, Steve. 1998. Island sizzle. *The Arizona Republic* September 25, page 1.

Zarbin, Earl.1995. Never retreat. Unpublished paper available at the Central Arizona Project library.

———. 1997. *Two sides of the river: Salt River Valley canals, 1867–1902.* Phoenix: Salt River Project.

Zygas, K. Paul, and Linda Johnson. 1995. *Frank Lloyd Wright: The Phoenix papers*, volumes I and II. Tempe: Herberger Center for Design Excellence, Arizona State University.

Index

176

New Urbanists, 63
New Visions for Metropolitan
    America, 55
Newlands Reclamation Act, 24
Noble, Dan, 35

Palmcroft, 15, 16
Papago Inner Loop, 51–52
Park Central Mall, 54
Parker Dam, 21
Period Revival architecture, 15
Phoenix
    annexation, 36–39, 49, 73, 98
    average temperatures, 89
    Broadacre City compared, 77
    downtown core, 57
    earliest shopping center, 41
    early impediments to growth,
        10–11
    embodiment of post-war
        dream, 48
    environmental deterioration,
        87–89
    fiscal integrity, 3
    founding, 9–11
    growth rate, 2, 36
    historic preservation programs,
        68–69
    a new vision, 144–151
    nomadic population, 3, 49
    population of 11, 14, 20, 38,
        48, 49
    poster child of sprawl, 2
    residential density, 69–71
    self-image, 59
    transformed by World War II,
        32–33
    urban form, 69
    view from the air, 1–2, 5
    water supply, 85–86
Phoenix Mountain Preserves, 101

Phoenix Planning Commission
    Concept 2000, 55
    creation, 15
    minor scandal, 54
    village cores, 54–58
Phoenix Street Railway Company,
    11–12, 41
Pima County, 86
Pinal County, 84, 86
Pinnacle West, 58
Planned Residental Development
    (PRD), 110–111
Portland, Oregon, UGB, 70–72, 92
Powell, John Wesley, 9, 22
President's Conference on Home
    Building and Home
    Ownership, 18
Publix Market, 41
Pueblo Grande, 10
Pulliam, Eugene, 52

Railroad, importance of access, 10
Ranch house, 39, 42–45, 147
Reclamation Service, 24
Residential density, 69–71, 75–78,
    107
Resolution Trust Corporation
    (RTC), 59
Retail
    shopping centers, 59–41, 54
    technology innovations, 80–81
Riley, Robert, 72–73
Rimza, Skip, 101
Roosevelt Dam, 24–25
Roosevelt, Theodore, 24
RTC see Resolution Trust
    Corporation (RTC)

Salt River, 26
    dams, 25
    irrigation, 9–10

Grady Gammage Jr. is an Arizona native who has practiced law in Phoenix since his graduation from Stanford Law School. He as spent the last 20 years dealing with land use, development, and growth issues; representing real estate development projects such as master-planned communities, high-rise buildings, regional shopping centers, and sprawling tracts of subdivisions; and consulting with cities and towns. In 1981, Mr. Gammage was instrumental in structuring Arizona's innovative Urban Lands Act, which allowed state trust lands to be released for private development. He has chaired the Phoenix Design Review Standards Committee twice, helping create mechanisms to regulate the aesthetics of commercial and residential development. He serves as an elected official as a board member of the Central Arizona Water Conservation District, and was president of that board from 1985–89. Mr. Gammage is also an adjunct professor at the Arizona State University Colleges of Architecture and Environmental Design and Law, where he teaches classes on land use regulation and on historic preservation planning.